A Mother's Rule of Life

Holly Pierlot

A Mother's Rule of Life

How to Bring Order to Your Home and Peace to Your Soul

SOPHIA INSTITUTE PRESS®
Manchester, New Hampshire

Sophia Institute Press®
Box 5284, Manchester, NH 03108
1-800-888-9344
www.sophiainstitute.com

Library of Congress Cataloging-in-Publication Data

Pierlot, Holly.
    A mother's rule of life : how to bring order to your home and peace to your soul / Holly Pierlot.
      p. cm.
    Includes bibliographical references.
    ISBN 1-928832-41-5 (pbk. : alk. paper)
    1. Mothers — Religious life. I. Title.
BV4529.18.P54 2004
248.8′431 — dc22   2004006556

04 05 06 07 08 09 10 9 8 7 6 5 4 3 2 1

*Dedicated to the Most Holy
and Immaculate Mother of God*

*Heartfelt gratitude to my husband, Philip, for a very
special marriage, for his wisdom and his never-ending
patience with me, both with this book and with my life.*

*Thank-yous and much love to my children, Anna,
Nicholas, Jessica, Luke, and Virginia for their special
love and help in making holy their mother.*

*To my editor, Todd Aglialoro, for his faith in me and for
always being available to help me, with kindness, insight, and
editorial expertise, no matter how often I pestered him.*

*To Fr. Joe Kane for his gentle encouragement and to
Fr. Blair Bernard for his stubborn insistence that I write
this book on the many occasions when I didn't want to.*

*To my own mother, Marg, who had more of an
influence on me than perhaps either of us ever realized;
and to all the mothers and friends who have walked
and talked with me about the Mother's Journey.*

Contents

Introduction

What does it mean to seek Christian perfection? A long time ago, I thought it meant perfect behavior — that if I just did what I was told, strictly followed all the rules, fervently prayed all the prayers, and spent a lot of time on aching knees in a quiet chapel somewhere, then I'd be "perfect." I'd *deserve* Heaven, really, because I was so good!

But the Pharisees thought this, too, and Jesus had some harsh words for those who merely conform to a set of external regulations and religious practices. No, Christian perfection is not about outward adherence to certain norms and laws. This has its place within the Christian life, and even an important place, but it's not the heart of perfection.

Later I developed a totally new concept of Christian perfection. It meant being a "saint" — someone who was engulfed in ecstasies, levitating high above the ground during prayer, receiving regular visions and apparitions. I was disappointed finally to learn this isn't the normal Christian calling! Such experiences are extraordinary phenomena, determined by God and given to select people at select times and places. So, no, Christian perfection is not about out-of-the-ordinary mystical experiences, although it can include these.

At another point, I thought Christian perfection meant being a nun, and so one day I shut the book *The Interior Castle* by St. Teresa of Avila, and I left it closed for a number of years, because her life and my life didn't have much in common. To be a wife and mother didn't seem synonymous with the holiness I was reading about there.

But somewhere along the way, I realized Christian perfection had to mean something else. It *had* to be something just anybody could do, because Jesus said, "You . . . must be perfect, as your heavenly Father is perfect,"[1] and he addressed this to all of us.

In my study, I came across a definition of *perfection* that finally made sense to me. Perfection is "union with God, which is possible in this world, consisting in and proportional to the degree of charity possessed and exercised. . . . When a [person] loves God with his whole heart, soul, mind, and strength, and his neighbor as himself for God's sake, then he is perfect."[2]

To seek perfection in this life is really *to seek union with God through love*.

Thus, Christian perfection can truly be the goal of *every* Christian life — not reserved to a few, nor tied up with an unrealistic view of what it means to be a saint. It doesn't mean you have to be a nun or a priest, a founder of some great congregation, or a silent contemplative in a hidden mountain retreat house. You don't have to be a miracle worker or someone in the public eye.

Perfection is for all of us, even for busy mothers stuck inside four walls, because all of us are called to love. We are *all* called to be saints, (although we are not all called to be canonized). We are

---

[1] Matt. 5:48.

[2] Donald Attwater, ed., *A Catholic Dictionary* (New York: The Macmillan Company, 1943), 399.

all called to holiness, which is nothing more that the perfection of love within us. And as mothers, there are lots of people we can love!

We don't have to wait until we get to Heaven to be united with God. Although eternity in Heaven is the *fulfillment* of our Christian life, that life is meant to be a process of steady growth in relationship with God. We're meant to know him *now*, to be in contact with him *now*, not at some point after Purgatory!

This goes for mothers, too. There isn't something inherent in our vocation that excludes us from a deep, intimate relationship with God. In fact, it's really quite the opposite. Since our lives as wives and mothers are a true *vocation* — a calling from God to us — God must want us to find him *within* our family life.

So although all is grace, a free gift of God, there is still much we can do to seek Christian perfection, no less than religious and priests and saints of the past and present. We can make ourselves available to God as best we can — to find ways to foster and dispose ourselves to God's presence in our lives, right now, amid the diapers, the bills, and the stomach flu.

And *this* is the purpose of a Mother's Rule of Life.

A Mother's Rule of Life

I Reach the Breaking Point

It was Saturday, January 1 of the year 2000. While the rest of the world was celebrating the dawn of the new millennium, I was pounding the kitchen table with my fist and issuing an ultimatum to my husband, Philip.

"We are sending the children to school . . . on Monday!" I had made up my mind. I just couldn't take it any longer, and he was not going to stop me.

We had been homeschooling for about four years, but things had gotten harder recently, and I was discouraged. In the last few months, since the newest baby had arrived, I felt increasingly overwhelmed by my responsibilities, and I had neither the time nor the energy to meet all the demands.

I had a daughter in fourth grade, Anna, who was just at the point where the whole world was opening up to her. I wanted to walk that journey with her and experience the wonder and the joy of the horizons of knowledge. I had a six-year-old son, Nicholas, who was learning to read, and I wanted to be able to cuddle up with him in a big, comfy chair to read and talk. My four-year-old daughter, Jessica, needed me to teach her patiently how to tie her shoes, and my feisty two-year-old son, Luke, just needed Mummy to crawl down on the floor with him, to tickle and roughhouse before giving him a tender hug and kiss. And I wanted simply to snuggle in silence with four-month-old Virginia, my love baby, who always smiled and cooed in my presence.

My heart was yearning to spend personal time with each of my children. But somehow I wasn't able to. My home seemed to be always in a shambles, the housework piling up and never ending. If I did a major clean, the house seemed to be a mess again before suppertime. If I spent time with one child, it seemed as if all the others needed my attention at the same moment. I felt as if I had three full-time jobs — my mothering, my housework, and my homeschooling — three full-time jobs, each impossible for me to accomplish.

On top of this, we were constantly low on funds; our family of seven was trying to live on my husband's modest teaching salary. It was customary for me to wait five or six months to make the most mundane purchases. Our van had broken down, and I was looking at another long, cold Canadian winter unable to get out of the house to visit friends or take a break with the kids.

I felt very alone. Philip was out all day at work, and I missed him. Day after day, I'd watch the clock, timing his arrival home and battling unreasonable feelings of resentment if he was the least bit late. During the day, most people on our street were at work or school or out and about, so there was no neighbor I could pop over to see (especially with five children). We didn't have mail delivery, so there wasn't even a postman to talk to! And to top it all off, I had no babysitter at that time.

Yes, the outlook was pretty dismal.

I remember walking around the kitchen, day after day, saying things like, "If I could just get someone to come in and help me get the house cleaned . . ." "If I could just get someone to come and watch the kids for a few hours so I could get the upstairs in order . . ." "If I could just buy more ready-made foods to cut back on my hours in the kitchen . . ." "Maybe, if I just went back to work . . ." These thoughts were constantly on my mind. I felt as if I was in a maze with high brick walls. I was running frantically down this passage and that, looking for a solution to even one of the difficulties, but turning corner after corner, I'd only run into another brick wall. I couldn't see a way out of the maze or over the walls.

I blamed homeschooling for this impossible state, and the only real solution I could see was to send the children to school. But it would have to be a secular school (there are no Catholic schools on Prince Edward Island, where we live), and this went against every conviction I had about the importance of a Christian education. I wasn't in the habit of dismissing my convictions, but I had reached my breaking point.

Hence the reason I sat at the table that first Saturday of the new millennium pounding my fist and issuing my ultimatum to my husband. Nothing was going to stop me in this, I said — not Philip, not even God! Philip sat calmly — in a state of controlled shock, I think — and said ever so gently, "Okay, we can send the children to school if you want, but I think you need to take a little time to consider whether this is best for our family."

"No! No! I don't want to reconsider! I've had it!" I hollered.

I have to hand it to Philip and the Holy Spirit at that moment, for they nonetheless both convinced me to postpone the decision for one week. Philip suggested that I take the week and bring it all to prayer, to see what God had to say to me. I very reluctantly agreed, although I was convinced there could be no change, since I had already been praying for ages and nothing had changed.

And so I began to pray, or should I say, to be *slightly open* to whatever it was the Lord wanted to show me, and on Tuesday, in a certain Scripture passage, Jesus spoke to me — or you might say he smacked me right across the head with a wet fish.

As he went ashore he saw a great throng; and he had compassion on them, and healed their sick. When it was evening, the disciples came to him and said, "This is a lonely place, and the day is now over; send the crowds away to go into the villages and buy food for themselves." Jesus said, "They need not go away; you give them something to eat." They said to him, "We have only five loaves here and two fish." And he said, "Bring them here to me." Then he ordered the crowds to sit down on the grass; and taking the five loaves and the two fish he looked up to Heaven, and blessed and broke and gave the loaves to the disciples, and the disciples gave them to the crowds. And they all ate and were satisfied. And they took up twelve baskets full of the broken pieces left over. And those who ate were about five thousand men, besides women and children.[3]

Here were the disciples, staring at a large crowd, seeing all the needs of the people, and knowing full well they couldn't meet those needs. The only solution they saw was to send the people away. And here I was, seeing the many tasks and needs of my home — for my children, my husband, homeschooling, not to mention myself — and the only solution I could see was to *send the children away*.

But when the disciples brought their concerns to Jesus, Jesus told them to feed the crowds themselves. The disciples must have been totally astonished, realizing the impossibility of the task before them. I, too, had realized the impossibility of the task. But Jesus wanted me to do it anyway.

And then it dawned on me. It wasn't the Apostles' meager five loaves and two fish that fed the crowds, but their offering combined

[3] Matt. 14:14-21.

with the blessing of Jesus. And Jesus was telling me to *give him my five loaves and two fish, my insignificant efforts, and he would bless them, and the needs of my family would be met.*

I was flying high at that moment, convinced again of my ability, united with grace, to meet the challenges of being home with my five children and homeschooling. A very real change took place in my heart that day, and I launched myself back into it with a new attitude. Now, I thought, everything would be okay.

But it wasn't.

A few months passed, and the situation didn't change. I still felt overwhelmed by my responsibilities. I still felt I didn't have time to devote to homeschooling as fully as I wanted to. My house was still a mess. We still had no money. Things were just as impossible as they had been before. I was perplexed: "Jesus, you told me you'd bless my efforts!" I struggled with disillusionment, and I felt lied to by the Lord. I knew this was impossible, but I was blind. I was becoming discouraged again. "Jesus, why aren't you helping me?"

Confronted with Order

Now it was the month of May and time for the Annual Homeschooling Conference near my home on Prince Edward Island, where I was scheduled to speak on the topic of "Babies, Toddlers, and Homeschooling." I had a carefully prepared talk written out — which I naturally forgot to bring with me. And as I sat through the morning sessions, my heart grew heavier. "Who am I to stand up there and tell anybody anything about homeschooling — I, who am failing so completely at it? What could I possibly say?" I dismissed as meaningless those points I could remember from my carefully prepared talk as meaningless; all logical counsels and practical hints, but advice that didn't really answer the question — that didn't answer *my* question.

And so when the time came for me to speak, I stood before the people present and announced with my opening words, "I come before you a failure." And I proceeded to tell them all the difficulties I had been experiencing, all the doubts and disillusionment. As I looked out over the small sea of faces, I found frowns of puzzlement on the faces of some women, those who didn't share what I was going through. But on the faces of others, I saw a nodding agreement, a deeply touching sign of sharing my experience, and I even saw a few tears in the corners of some eyes. I saw women who knew the struggles and the suffering, and I saw them soothed and consoled by the very simple knowledge that they were not the only ones, that someone intimately understood their plight.

I wrapped it up by saying, "And so the Lord has promised he will bless my efforts, and I guess I stand before you now, just waiting for him to do so." I returned quietly to my seat.

Then it was time for the next speaker. Alice got up there, bubbling with excitement and energy — energy I hadn't felt in years and was sure I'd never get back. I was immediately suspicious!

She began her bubbly presentation by talking about the joys of home management based on the something called the Managers of Their Homes (MOTH) program. She seemed to have it all together; the only thing she couldn't quite find the time to do, she said, was to dust the top of the piano! The audience members sat there with their jaws dropped in disbelief and astonishment. I spent half of her talk sitting there, trying to discredit her. "She must not have many children," I thought. Well, no, she had four. "Her children must all be older than mine," I countered. Well, no, I discovered, her children were approximately the same ages as mine. "This program must be really new, and she's still in the honeymoon stage," I argued. Well, no, she had been successfully following it for more than three months, which was quite a feat in my estimation. Every one of my attempts to discredit her in my own mind was shot down, and so I settled in to listen reluctantly to what she had to say.

She talked next about schedules. Oh, here we go! I had already tried schedule after schedule, and they fell through every single time. Besides which, I wasn't a schedule-type person; I didn't *want* to live every day the same, or I'd go nuts. The MOTH program did, however, have an interesting twist that I had never thought of before. I had always scheduled myself and the children into the same activities, so all of us would do housecleaning together, or recess, or story time, or whatever. But the MOTH program scheduled *each* person of the family separately so that each person might be doing something very different in the same time frame, and worked out these individual schedules in harmony with each of the others.

Now *here* was a new, unique, and creative idea! But no, I still wasn't interested, for down in my heart, my level of discouragement told me it would never work. And I didn't have any energy left to try something new anyway.

The following day, on a Sunday afternoon, I was sitting in my chair in the living room, frustrated again. The kids were all around me, each clamoring for my attention: "Mummy, can you play cards with me?" "No, I want her to play with *me!*" "Mummy, you told me you'd read this story!" "Mummy, can we go visit someone instead?" In addition, the entire house was decked in the decorating style I called Early Colonial Chaos: socks, shoes, blankets, toys, books, papers, pillows, and cat fluff graced the living-room floor; food-caked dishes from the night before were piled high in the sink beside the breakfast dishes; laundry formed a voluminous mountain in the bathroom; and the bedrooms — well, I had just closed my eyes when I came downstairs.

"I might not like schedules," I thought to myself then, "but I certainly can't stand this either!" I reasoned, if God has given me a job to do, and he is a God of order, and if a schedule helps to bring about order, and my present ways aren't working, then perhaps I should think about a schedule. Old objections reappeared in my mind: I'm too "spontaneous" to be "limited" by a schedule, I thought. Schedules are so . . . *limiting*.

But this time I had a response.

Schedules might be limiting, I countered, *but disorder is more limiting*. My cherished spontaneity was pointless when I didn't have the time or energy to enjoy it. I was resolved to bring order where there had been chaos, and if it took a schedule, then so be it.

A Complete Commitment to My State of Life

By Sunday night, I was ready. I had assessed what I needed. I had assessed what the kids needed. I had assessed what the house, my husband, and the cats needed. It was confusing, and more than a little daunting. But on Monday, I began the implementation of a very basic schedule that tried to cover the major needs.

Wham! It worked! On Day One!

By noon that first day, the laundry had been done and put back in the drawers; all the kids' schoolwork was finished, and the house hadn't been demolished because they'd been constructively engaged in other things, and the toddler hadn't cried from lack of attention all morning.

By suppertime that first day, the house was still clean. In fact, cleaner. Five-year-old Jessica had mopped the living room, the hall, and the classroom. Six-year-old Nicki had shaken the mats in the entry, swept, and put the mats back. Eight-year-old Anna had baked muffins for the next two days' breakfasts. In addition, the kids had enjoyed half an hour of quiet reading time, played on the computer, built numerous Lego creations, spent an hour outside, and each produced a work of art. And they'd topped it off with a well-deserved *Magic School Bus* video (it's science, you know).

By bedtime, children, house, and Mummy were all clean and happy. Imagine! But the clincher was — and remember, I like to be spontaneous and free — the clincher was when I found that I had hours throughout the day to spend thinking and planning my new schedule. Hours that were going to be a constant in my life: hours a day to rest, or develop my home business, or clean an attic, or plant a garden, or to cuddle kids . . . or to be spontaneous.

At prayer that evening, it dawned on me: the answer to my perplexity about why Jesus had not "helped me as he'd promised." I understood that Jesus is perfectly willing to bless my efforts, but first *he had to have efforts to bless*. I had to do all in my power to fulfill my obligations. I had to give a full five loaves and two fish — not three loaves, not two loaves. I had to apply *all of me* to the task and mission I was called to be and do, not haphazardly, but fully, methodically, completely. *Jesus was asking for the dedication of my entire self to my vocation.*

I understood that this dedication went beyond just my housework and could not be limited to home management. What Jesus wanted from me was to pull together all I had learned from him and from my study about what it means to be a Christian and a woman, a wife and a mother, and a member of the Church and of society. He wanted me to analyze my vocation, to see what he was calling me to, and then to implement it in my life. He was talking about a Rule of Life that goes far beyond a housekeeping schedule; nothing short of a complete and proper ordering of every aspect of my life.

I knew then what Jesus wanted. But I had no idea where it would take me.

Chapter 2

⁓

A Rule of Life

A complete and proper ordering of my whole life? That's a tall order! Just how was I to go about it? I found my answer in the concept of a Rule of Life.

A Rule of Life is a traditional Christian tool for ordering one's vocation. Found most often in religious community life, a Rule can also be used by laypeople — whose state in life is no less a calling from God. It consists primarily in the examination of one's vocation and the duties it entails, and the development of a schedule for fulfilling these responsibilities in a consistent and orderly way.

When a woman has been called to become a nun, in addition to taking vows of poverty, chastity, and obedience, she agrees to follow the Rule of the community. There are set norms and routines for community and private prayer, meals, chores, recreation, dress, house rules, and the exercise of the specific apostolate of the order. These are all essential to the smooth flow of daily life. It simply wouldn't do to have nuns bickering over who has to wash the bathroom floor or who has to make supper that night!

The Rule brings order: "a happy disposition of things . . . a multitude reduced in some wise to unity."[4] That was just what I

---

[4] Attwater, *Catholic Dictionary*, 376.

wanted: a "happy disposition," and to reduce all the overwhelming tasks of motherhood into a nice, single unit of work I could handle. And in my mind, I couldn't see any extreme difference between a religious community and a family community: there's still the mother abbess (the mom), and the postulants and novices (the little ones the mom needs to raise), and the professed sisters (the older children who can help out). The nuns all need to eat and sleep and dress and pray and do their work. So do all of us in the family!

But there was something else I found intriguing about the whole notion of a Rule of Life: that it was also supposed to lead me to *holiness*.

Hmmm . . . wouldn't that be something? A happy home *and* getting closer to God all at the same time! The reasoning is that since our vocation is a specific call of God — a particular mission we have been given on earth — living out this mission is to do God's will in our lives. To do God's will because he asks it of us, out of love for him, is to advance on the road to holiness, to seek perfection. And so I realized that a mother's Rule of Life would, ideally, serve as a tool for getting my life pulled together as well as a means to achieve holiness through my vocation as a wife and mother.

The Practical Aspect of a Rule

A Rule of Life is not just a schedule, not just a collection of activities organized into a set pattern for efficient repetition. A Rule is *an organization of everything that has to do with your vocation*, based on a hierarchy of the priorities that define the vocation and done with the intent to please God. It deals with the *essential responsibilities* of your state of life, organized to ensure their fulfillment. The activities worked into the Rule are determined by the specific calling, charism, and apostolate of the person living the Rule. This is the practical aspect of a Rule.

For an example from religious life, let's look at Bl. Mother Teresa's Missionaries of Charity. The daily schedule of the sisters is quite simple:

4:30-5:00	*Rise and get cleaned up*
5:00-6:30	*Prayers and Mass*
6:30-8:00	*Breakfast and clean-up*
8:00-12:30	*Work for the poor*
12:30-2:30	*Lunch and rest period*
2:30-3:00	*Spiritual reading and meditation*
3:00-3:15	*Tea break*
3:15-4:30	*Adoration*
4:30-7:30	*Work for the poor*
7:30-9:00	*Dinner and clean-up*
9:00-9:45	*Night prayers*
9:45	*Bedtime*

This basic schedule is consistent day by day, week by week. The two primary goals of the Missionaries of Charity are love of God and love of neighbor, as found in the poorest of the poor. Their time is allotted to fulfill these two aims. Note how the schedule covers a full seven hours for work with the poor and four hours of prayer every day. In addition, all their meals, chores, study, recreation, and even rest are accounted for.

I couldn't see why this wouldn't work for me as an at-home mom, or for one who might work outside the home, for that matter. We all share the same need for sleep and rest, meals, prayers, and work every day. Why couldn't I just write in my specific family and vocational duties in place of the sisters' work for the poor, since so much else was the same?

A Mother's Rule of Life

It struck me that many people already incorporate the schedule element of a Rule in their daily routines. Adults at work have schedules (whether they're aware of the routine or not) of work time, coffee breaks, travel time, and so on. Children in school follow class schedules, with set times for recess, meals, free time, and bus waits. Surely I, as an at-home mom, was not in an impossible situation if even school kids could follow a basic schedule.

There was hope! The question now was not, "*Can* I do this?" as once seemed perfectly reasonable to me, but "*How* will I do this?"

There Are Reasons Behind a Rule

Let's look again to Mother Teresa and her sisters. We noted that their vocation is to love God and love their neighbor, as found in the poorest of the poor. Therefore, their Rule is an examination of what this means, and their schedule is a reflection of their calling. Time is allotted according to what is important and specific to their charism.

When Mother Teresa began writing her Rule, she didn't begin with the schedule. Instead she began writing out the "principles and spiritual goals" that defined the mission of the Missionary of Charity. "Our aim is to quench the great thirst of the love of Jesus Christ by our evangelical vows, to dedicate ourselves freely to serving the poorest of the poor according to the example and teaching of our Lord, and thus to proclaim in a special way the Kingdom of God," she said. "Our specific mission is to work for the salvation and the sanctification of the poorest of the poor."[5]

It was only after Mother Teresa had first defined specifically what she was doing and why she was going to do it, that she next

[5] Lush Gjergji, *Mother Teresa: Her Life, Her Works* (Hyde Park, New York: New City Press, 1991), 49.

drew up a simple schedule based on that mission — a schedule in which the bulk of the sisters' time would be spent in prayer and service to the poor. We see, then, that the practical element of a Rule is a *reflection of the aims and mission of our vocation*, which should determine how we spend our time.

Now, I had tried schedules before and had failed. Was that because I was trying to order my life according to goals that didn't reflect what my calling as a Christian, a wife, and a mother demanded? Was the stress I had been experiencing the result of an imbalance in my priorities? Seeing how I was so often confused about everything, did I even know what my primary daily duties were supposed to be? After all, a Rule of Life deals primarily with *essential responsibilities*. How could I know whether I was giving these the primacy they deserve?

The Five Priorities of the Married Vocation

With all my research, I never found an example of a Rule of Life written by a layperson. Most Rules I came across were of religious orders. So I had to ask myself: what was it about my vocation that was unique to married life? Where could I turn for help in defining and developing a Rule specifically for mothers? I remembered a wise old priest telling me, early on in my marriage, about the Five "Ps" of Married Life — the five priorities of the married vocation:

> First P = Prayer
> Second P = Person
> Third P = Partner
> Fourth P = Parent
> Fifth P = Provider

The priest said that every woman called to be a wife and mother has certain obligations that must be fulfilled; true "duties" in that they can't be ignored nor neglected. They're not optional for a married woman, regardless of her other involvements. A mother trying to forgo any of these five priorities would be like a doctor abandoning his office to go down the street and practice law. Whether or not we knew what we were signing up for when we said, "I do," these obligations are ours by virtue of our married vocation.

The priest explained that these must be ranked according to importance, and that many marriages can get "out of order" when a lesser P is given priority over a higher P. For example, he said, in his experience, husbands tend to place their provider role above all else, often spending too much time (in mind as well as in body) at the office, while women tend to place their parenting role above all else, often not leaving enough time for their own needs, or their husbands'.

Now, given that the five Ps are often interrelated, we don't have to differentiate between them with mathematical precision. I shouldn't ignore a wounded child just because I'm saying my Rosary, which is a higher P. On the other hand, ordinarily speaking, I wasn't to let the demands of housework and child-raising lead me to neglect my prayer life. As a general guide, the five Ps are an indication of what God wants us to concern ourselves with as mothers, and he expects a conscious effort to include all the priorities and work them out in a reasonable fashion.

So, I began to order my life according to the proper hierarchy of priorities.

• *The First P: Prayer.* God was calling to me get my personal life in order by establishing, as top priority, the care of my soul and body. The use of my time was to reflect the importance of these activities.

This meant that I had to put first things first, and the very first thing was God. Instead of never finding enough time for God in the midst of everything else, I had to work everything else around God. This meant that I determined which prayers and practices I thought were basic to Christian living and worked out a basic schedule for them. I also created a set program for Christian study and spiritual reading, Mass, Adoration and Confession, days for silence in retreat, and meeting with my spiritual director. I also drew up a basic family prayer routine to help my children put God first, too.

• *The Second P: Person.* Next, I needed to ensure that I was caring for my basic physical needs. So I set about determining how much sleep I felt my body needed to keep me refreshed, how much exercise I needed, what types of foods and vitamin supplements I needed, and so on. I likewise considered my mental and emotional health.

• *The Third P: Partner.* Now, Philip is a grown man and capable of taking care of himself! But I understood that a solid, loving marriage is the bedrock of family life, and so the next allotment of my time and energy had to be directed at my partner, my husband. So I set aside my evenings to be available to him first and foremost, before all other activities.

• *The Fourth P: Parent.* I had considered my children's physical and spiritual needs when I worked out my own, but now I needed to focus on how to love them in a conscious, consistent way. I tried to be more available to them throughout the day, and soon discovered that it wasn't just my physical availability that was called for; my children also needed me to be *mentally* available to them — to be fully attentive to them when I was with them. I had to tone down thoughts of all the projects that filled my head and make more casual time to talk and laugh and simply *be* with them.

Regarding my call to educate my children, I realized prayer and Mass and faith discussion and good stories of saints and virtue were at least as important as their daily math lesson. As such, I began to work on developing their faith life a little more regularly and encouraging prayer and more frequent reception of the sacraments.

• *The Fifth P: Provider.* Both my husband and I are called to provide for our family. Philip provides in his way by going to work and earning a paycheck. I provide in my way by caring for, maintaining, and repairing (as much as possible) our home and our resources, and if time permits, in earning a little extra income on a casual basis to help out financially. For working women, the duties of their jobs would figure in here as well.

I decided to get the house in order and set out to create housework routines that took care of the basic daily, weekly, and monthly needs of the home. It's amazing how housework diminishes, and cleaning time lessens, when the home is regularly maintained instead of allowing things to pile up!

I also made room for home and garden projects and a few income-producing projects. And after all this, I found I still had hours a day of free time, which I could spend in volunteer work, in family time, or in some other service to my church or community.

My Initial Mother's Rule

So how did my Rule look, once I got everything organized? It was really quite simple. It had both a daily and a weekly format.

From Monday to Friday, I rose at 6:45, fed the cats, put on the coffee, and spent the remaining time until the children got up, at 7:30, with Scripture.

From 7:30 to 9:00, we dressed and cleaned up, tidied the upstairs, prepared and ate breakfast, cleaned the kitchen, put on laundry, dispensed vitamins, changed the baby, and brushed our teeth.

From 9:00 to 10:15, we prayed and did schoolwork. (Two to three mornings a week, we now attend Mass.)

At 10:15, I sent the kids out for a recess, and I threw on another load of laundry, grabbed a cup of coffee, and said mid-morning prayers, usually psalms or a chaplet.

At 10:45, the kids came back in, and we did more schoolwork. The littlest ones played with toys or watched a video at this time.

From 11:45 to 12:30, the kids tidied up, each child taking a downstairs room while I made lunch; we ate and cleaned the kitchen. I put on another laundry load.

From 12:30 to 1:30, the children had a quiet reading/play time in their rooms while I said my Rosary or did some spiritual reading or reflection.

At 1:30, I attended to housework or projects, finished any homeschooling, scheduled visits and appointments, worked in the garden, or sewed, depending on the day. The kids usually spent some time in an independent school project, then played with the little ones, did computer work, watched an educational video of some kind, sewed or painted or built Lego creations.

At 3:30, I sent the children out for another recess, and I had a coffee/recreation break.

At 4:00, I entered the kitchen. Until supper was on the table at 5:30, I spent my time doing meal prep and any baking for the next day, folding laundry, unloading the dishwasher, setting the table, making Philip's lunch for the next day, and setting up the coffee maker for the next morning. The older kids had free time with their little brother and sister. At 5:15, they each tidied a room once more and took all the family laundry up to the right rooms before sitting down for supper.

After supper, we followed a little policy: no one leaves the kitchen until it's clean — including my husband. And so usually within five or ten minutes, it was finished. (Later on, I switched to itemized chore charts in the kitchen for each person. Over time, we found this took too long, so while they're still posted and can be done independently by the children if the need arises, we all usually just do it together nice and quickly.)

After that, I was free to go for a walk, visit the Blessed Sacrament, and come back and play a little piano. The kids, meanwhile, put their clothes away, had some free time, or bathed and got ready for bed.

At 7:30, we had family prayer, and by 8:00, it was bedtime for the kids. I've since developed a staggered bedtime to accommodate the various ages of the children.

For the remainder of the evening I was available to Philip, or I worked on sewing projects or other interests. I also took some time here for any faith or vocation study. I'd occasionally watch a show.

Somewhere around 10:00 on most evenings, I prepped for the next day. I emptied the dishwasher, quickly tidied up what was left to do downstairs, put away my laundry if Philip hadn't already done it, and took care of personal hygiene. I'd spend a few minutes in prayer and reading before bed at 10:30.

On Saturdays, I dropped the time schedule, made sure I got morning, afternoon, and evening prayer in, and maintained the tidiness and kitchen and laundry. The children got to Confession on these Saturdays, either once or twice a month. The rest of the time was mine. Every other Saturday, I had my Mother's Day Out. For Sundays, on the advice of my spiritual director, I was to have only three goals: lots of God, lots of family, and lots of rest! That was easy! On Sunday night, we all quickly tidied up before family prayer.

A Rule of Life

That was the daily schedule. There were weekly things as well. Monday and Friday, I had a Holy Hour in the perpetual-Adoration chapel in our community. Fridays we cleaned the downstairs — dusted, vacuumed, and mopped — which was always followed by Movie Night with soda and chips. Every other Saturday morning, when I wasn't on my day out, we cleaned the upstairs, including changing the sheets. Philip and I had a biweekly cenacle at that time. Confession was every other week on my day out. I met with my spiritual director once a month. Thursday evenings I balanced the checkbook and paid the bills, and Wednesdays before the bi-weekly payday, I defrosted and cleaned our aging fridge and freezer, making shopping lists as I went. I arranged with other home-schooling friends to "swap" kids one or two afternoons a week. On those days when my children were out, I'd do errands, keep appointments, or work on special home projects. Anything that I could routinize I did. It saved me having to arrange everything all the time.

I also allowed for emergencies and other realities to interfere. I'd move into "maintenance mode" on days when a child was sick or I had been up all night or company came unexpectedly. Then, I'd simply ensure that the essentials got done, even if it cut into my free time. To me, the essentials were prayer, meals, laundry and tidy-up, and for the children to do their math and spelling if they weren't sick. Also, if the whole family got stressed and developed cabin fever, as can happen when you homeschool, I included as part of my Rule the ability to drop everything, and spend the day doing interesting science experiments or getting out of the house for a change of pace. My family's personal needs came first.

After all, *the Rule is a tool, not a tyrant*. The schedule is made for the family, not the family for the schedule. The only thing I watched out for was that this bare-bones schedule did not become the norm. I had to learn to be flexible, but not so flexible that I reasoned myself right out of a schedule again!

These basic time frames, which met all the needs of our daily life, have been more or less a constant ever since I began my Rule. The actual times are pretty consistent, although I'm not as rigid about starting lunch at exactly 12:00 now that I'm used to my Rule and know how long things take. One thing became very important: I had to allow plenty of time for the accomplishment of the various tasks; otherwise I'd get too stressed.

In the beginning, I spent a good deal of time adjusting and assessing what was working and what wasn't, and every autumn, I adjust the Rule to meet the growing needs and abilities of my children. As they've grown, they now help out in the kitchen, preparing meals. Where once I did all the cooking, Anna is now perfectly capable with instructions to make the family supper a couple of evenings a week. She and the others also help with lunch prep. I assign them the work that any of us can do, and I do the work that only I can do. That way, I'm freer to fulfill other, more detailed tasks such as making doctor's appointments or marking math schoolwork.

A Time for Every Task

Over the course of many months, I worked out the practicalities of my Mother's Rule and, step by step, implemented them in my life. I remember that first summer, as Philip began his vacation and we were discussing how he'd spend his time. I had things in such order that I could honestly look at him and say, "Aside from bathing the little ones after supper, there's no real housework for you to do. Perhaps you might like to focus on other things around the house, or build that veranda." Imagine — can you think of any woman in her right mind who would tell her husband that she didn't need any help around the house? But it was true. Things were running so smoothly that I didn't really need any extra help.

The very first thing I noticed was there was *order* in my home. (The very first thing Philip noticed was that the laundry was put away in the drawers everyday, and he didn't have to hunt for socks!) The house was clean. There was a place for everything. There was a time for everything.

As a result, it *freed my mind from a thousand cares and concerns*. Whereas before I would stare around the house, wondering which task to tackle first, and as I worked on one, a hundred new ones would come in to worry me, now I knew exactly when every task in my home was going to be done. Knowing that tidy-up came just before supper made me stop tidying up constantly throughout the day. Knowing that the laundry was going to be done in the morning stopped the pressure of seeing dirty laundry in the basket every evening. Knowing that the floor was to be mopped on Friday made me not so concerned with a messy floor on Thursday night. Because there was a time and place for all, the moments I didn't have scheduled for chores became "free." I stopped thinking about all the responsibilities I had weighing on me and was able to concentrate on the present moment, fully and freely.

I found my Mother's Rule brought greater *balance* to my life. Whereas before there seemed to be a never-ending list of chores to get done, now I found I had ample time for quiet or reading or a card game with the kids. Since the five Ps each had significant needs to balance, no particular aspect of life outweighed the other. Each need in my vocation and my personal life was given its fair share of my time. Hence, I found a greater variety of pursuits in my daily life as well as the discovery of *real* free time. Life was not *all* work or *all* play, but a healthy interweaving of both. This reduced my stress level significantly and led to greater personal satisfaction with being at home.

And the children? The children were thriving. They stopped living what I call the "TV Sitcom Syndrome," wherein, having no set plan for the evening, they were tempted to watch aimlessly one sitcom after another for lack of anything more meaningful to do. Now, instead, they had a plan for their days. High-quality home-schooling, housework, leisure, prayer, and personal time were all really happening. Nicki, my oldest son, would come to me and say things like, "You know, Mummy, I really feel good when I do my work!" and, "You know, Mummy, if we just *keep* it tidy, there's less work to do on cleaning day. Why don't we just do that?" Yes, my six-year-old genius!

There was another benefit to the Rule that I never would have predicted: it *cut down on bickering and arguments* with the children. Because there was a time for everything now, I wasn't constantly interfering with their free time to call them to do chores. Free time really meant free time, and the groans of annoyance (for the most part) ended, because they knew what was expected of them and when it was expected. The Rule and its flow of work and rest, play and prayer was a *motivator* for them to finish their work; and they had the time they needed to do it well.

Also, to know that chore time would be done in fifteen minutes was to be able to put it into perspective. They knew there was a limit to the nasty stuff Mummy was going to assign — for suffering is always lessened when you realize it isn't going to be eternal!

Spiritual Benefits of a Mother's Rule

So often in life I've wondered what God's will for me was. Through the use of my Rule, I've learned that God's will isn't so mysterious. I believe there are three main things he wants from each of us: first, to love him and obey his commands; second, to do our daily duties according to the state of life we've been called to; and third, to be open to the inspirations of the Holy Spirit in our daily lives.

As I began to live my Rule, I became excited by the very fact that day by day, and moment by moment, I was trying to fulfill God's will in my life. As a nun vows obedience to her superiors, I was practicing obedience to the demands of my vocation as reflected in my daily duties. I was obeying God with each and every action I performed, right down to loading the dishwasher and feeding the cats.

The freedom of spirit I experienced was astonishing. Oftentimes, when things had gone wrong in the past, I would rack my brain, trying to figure out whether I had done something wrong, or whether I was somehow displeasing God. But now, knowing that I was doing my best to live out His plan for me, I found a sense of peace in the face of trials. I was aware that if problems occurred, it wasn't because I was just being slack!

This also helped me tolerate any dryness I experienced in my prayer as well. To know that I was doing all I could to spend time in prayer, I began to understand that spiritual dryness was not something I could do much about, that it rested in the hands of the Lord. It became easier to trust that, if I needed it, God would indeed send some consolation.

In addition, a Mother's Rule is sanctifying, because by it *we do what we ought to do*. It's a great means of mortification.

What is mortification? Due to Original Sin and compounded by our own sinful acts, our natures are out of whack. We have disordered passions and desires for things that aren't good for us, and tendencies to sin rather than to virtue. Hence, while God is always acting through grace to restore order to our disordered souls and bodies, we must cooperate with him.[6] We respond to this grace through mortification, by dying to our disordered selves; by doing our part to tame our selfishness and sinfulness and choose the real good that God puts before us.

Now, you may have a pretty tainted view of what mortification entails, as I once did. I remember reading about how St. Francis ran and threw himself into a thorn bush to conquer a temptation. I read about St. Rose of Lima, who slept on a bed of broken glass. Many medieval saints wore hairshirts that constantly irritated their skin. But such forms of mortification are extraordinary and not even desirable for the average Christian.

Following our Rule, doing what we ought for God and our families, provides more than enough mortification to help God purify us! It is just as difficult, because of our own sinful nature, to do what we ought — to get out of bed on time, to eat healthful meals, to exercise, or even to clean that gross little area behind the toilet. Even these mundane efforts to do what is good and true and to oppose our disordered tendencies and attractions is true mortification. It's also known by many other names: self-control, self-discipline, or as St. John of the Cross calls it, the Active Night. It is our wills, acting in sacrificial love, doing all because God asks it of us, that enable God to change our hearts to love in a deeper way.

This inevitably leads to virtue for, as the *Catechism of the Catholic Church* tells us, "human virtues [are] acquired by . . . deliberate acts and by a perseverance ever renewed in repeated efforts [that] are purified and elevated by divine grace. With God's help, they forge character and give facility in the practice of the good. The virtuous man is happy to practice them."[7] The very action of

[6] Cf. Col. 1:24.
[7] Par. 1810.

doing our duties and following our Rule sanctifies us, or makes us holy. It even makes doing good *easier,* for as we develop good habits, the work we do ceases to be so arduous. I remember, at one point, not even being sure I was following my Rule because it seemed to have become so natural. I would go to my schedule and check to see whether I was forgetting something!

I realized, too, that my Mother's Rule also helps my children in this regard. Not only does it bring physical order and the practice of good daily habits to their lives, but also, they witness Mummy's good example. As Pope Paul VI stated, the most effective form of evangelization is the witness of our lives, and only secondly, the words we use to explain the reason for our hope.

A Rule Is More than a Schedule

It's easy to see the practical benefits of a Rule of Life. Things are in order, and life can be lived very efficiently. But if we stop there, focusing on the schedule and seeking *only* efficiency, we miss the point of a Rule. Take, for example, a high-powered business executive who may very well have a truly rigorous schedule, balanced in most ways, and who may follow it religiously. Perhaps he meets with his advisors at exactly 9:00 a.m., schedules financial conferences for 10:30 sharp, meets a prospective client for lunch at noon, and assesses the daily profits at 1:00 p.m. every day, like clockwork. Could we truly say that he was following a Rule of Life?

No, there's a deeper and more fundamental level to a Rule of Life that distinguishes it from a mere schedule: the intent and aim of following the Rule. A Rule followed for the practical benefits alone is not a Rule of Life; it is a schedule. Duties attended to grudgingly or with reluctance do not make a Rule, for a Rule of Life must be lived *as a response to the call of God.*

A Mother's Rule of Life

In a Mother's Rule, all that we do is done because God asks it of us. It is to accept and embrace my vocation because God wants me to, whether out of an initial sense of obedience to him or, later, simply because I love him, and to suffer the possibly ongoing struggle to adjust my attitudes and outlook toward his vision for my life, is the very heart of the Rule. *It is to do all that he asks, because he asks it, out of love for him.*

And so, to bring God into every part of my day, every time I looked at the schedule to see what was next, I simply said a little prayer and asked him to be with me and bless the next allotment of time. This, as well as my scheduled prayer times, made me much more aware of his ongoing presence throughout my day. And soon, I began to be able to do things with him, and for him, like folding that baby sleeper just so.

The Time to Start Your Rule Is Now

Now, seeing as how I was already about ten years into my married life, I didn't have the leisure to spend a couple of years examining my vocation so thoroughly that I could write up a perfect Rule that would launch me into perfect order and perfect holiness immediately. So, I decided I had to just *start*, anywhere, and study as I went. I established the initial schedule, which brought about balance and order and which then left me open to study my vocation with more depth as I went.

Interestingly, I later found out that this is what nuns do anyway! When a novice enters a community, she immediately begins to follow the schedule of the Rule to align her activity with that of the rest of the sisters. But, for the next few years, she also studies the Rule and its principles and aims in order more fully to spiritualize her daily routine and enhance the meaning of the sometimes mundane things she might find herself doing.

And as Mother Teresa once said when teaching her sisters about their Rule, it was the *spirit* of the Rule that was to be stressed. And so, while I had the basic schedule in order, I began to call to mind what I had learned over the years about the five Ps and began consciously to work on them. I needed to understand better the spirit of *my* Mother's Rule, to grasp the significance of why I was doing all this.

I'd like to share with you, then, some of what I have learned about my vocation as a Christian wife and mother, in the events and circumstances of my own life. Along the way, I'll offer some basic advice on how you can develop your own Mother's Rule. And as the Church has always stressed the importance of the spiritual dimension of the Rule, its very heart, I'd like to show you how I have come to understand the goal of holiness as it can be sought and lived in the married vocation.

Chapter 3

⮜

The First P: Prayer

Immersed in the busyness and difficulties of life, as mothers we naturally tend to focus on the practicalities. It's easy to forget that we have a deeper calling when the dog is barking, the phone is ringing, the stove timer is beeping, and the baby is crying. Because we live in the world, it becomes very easy to forget about our ultimate purpose or to see any deeper meaning or reality in life. But we do have a calling to something far greater than what we see around us.

This path to God has many stages, and God leads each of us in a unique way to him. He often reveals himself to us gradually, almost maddeningly so at times. But we're not helpless. There are things we can do to deepen our relationship with God. The spirit of the first P, then, is to look into our own lives, see where God has led us so far, and learn what we ought to do to make ourselves more available to his direct and personal intervention in our lives.

Sometimes this means simply realizing we need him.

The Something Search

It was so beautiful, the bright sun and the cloudless blue sky. I was sitting on a child's swing on a rolling hill in Cape Breton, Nova Scotia, a warm breeze caressing my back and swirling around my legs. The tall grass danced gently around me. The reflection of the sun glistened like a thousand diamonds on the harbor down below. Some birds were singing and getting ready to fly south for the winter. It was a picture postcard in every way.

So beautiful outside, but inside I was wracked with despair.

I was only twenty-one, but I felt old, worn out, used, and as empty as an old kettle drum. Something was missing in my life, and I didn't know what it was. I had been on a "something search" for five years — trying to find *something* to fill my heart. I had rejected the life of my parents, because I had found no satisfaction there and had rebelled into a life of pleasing myself in any way I could. But the more I tried to fill myself, the emptier I became.

I had been on the road for a couple of years, singing with a band. I had been raised a Catholic, but had never met God. I believed he existed, I even believed in the Catholic Church, but I just couldn't see what difference it made. Christianity to me was just a series of rules and restrictions on my freedom. I was tired of "thou shalts" and "thou shalt nots" and having someone else dictate to me how to live. Clearly, this didn't satisfy the deep needs of my heart.

Just a few short years earlier, I had entered the confessional for what I thought would be the very last time. "Father," I declared, "I can't see the point in this." The priest asked me to explain. I continued, "Here I come to Confession, over and over again, confessing the very same sins and getting nowhere. The reality is, I have no intention of stopping the sins I'm committing because I can't see any good reason for doing so. I will not be coming back." The priest let out a quiet groan and said, finally, "At least you have integrity." He proceeded to bless me, and I walked out for what I thought was for good.

So, set loose in the music business (a profession not known for its virtue!), I did whatever I wanted for the next couple of years and cast off the moral and social norms of my childhood in favor of "freedom." I indulged in whatever pastimes looked fun and exciting and which I thought would make me happy, but nothing was able to fill the hole in my heart. That warm afternoon on the swing was a turning point — the day I decided there was nothing left to try, nothing left to go after, no answer to my "something search."

Within a few weeks, I had joined a new band in Halifax. I was staying at the drummer's apartment and slept on a mattress inside a large walk-in closet. One night, as I lay there in the darkness, looking through the patio doors at the fog, all orange from the streetlight, I decided I had nothing to lose. I turned on my back and addressed the ceiling:

"God, if you're there, I figure it's your responsibility to show yourself to me. I've done everything I can with my life here. If you want me to get to know you, you need to reveal yourself to me; and it's up to you, because if you are God, I'm sure you can find a way." And then I rolled over and went to sleep.

Weeks passed. I was home on break and sat down one evening to watch a movie about the aftermath of a nuclear war. It was so depressing, so desolate, so hopeless that I simply couldn't believe the world would end this way. An idea came to me, and I went upstairs to my room and dug out a Bible that belonged to my aunt. I turned immediately to the Book of Revelation and began reading. I read all night long, well into the early hours of dawn, and by the time I closed my eyes for sleep, I had found the Something.

God had stirred my heart while I read Scripture that night in a real and personal way, perhaps in an extraordinary way, and I fell asleep content that I had found God. After such a long and difficult search, I knew that my answers would somehow come through him. It was only later that I realized that the search itself was really a form of prayer; my heart had been rising up with a question to my Creator without even consciously knowing whom I was asking. I believe God had been working in me all along, in the very midst of my discontent.

The Religious Impulse Within Us

"What is it?" "What is missing from my life?" Many people today experience this void as well and, as I did, try to fill it with worldly distractions: money, travel, power, pleasure, human recognition and fame, career success, sex and drugs, hobbies and diversions, even "causes" and volunteer work; the list goes on. But nothing fits the bill, because this essential restlessness is a desire for our hearts to be filled with something more than we can attain on our own: God himself. As St. Augustine said, "Our hearts were made for you, O Lord, and they are restless until they rest in you."

As mothers, we, too, can quite innocently get caught up in the distractions of daily life and not even notice that our relationship with God is slipping. We suddenly realize we haven't really prayed for a while. Even with the best intentions, this can happen regularly if we haven't consciously set aside time, and we wonder why things become stressful or we lack energy and vigor in fulfilling our duties.

Sometimes, our own restlessness with the often mundane tasks of mothering can tempt us to seek meaning outside of our calling. I know I've had any number of fads and fashions, temporary projects that consumed my attention again and again throughout my mothering career. We can find ourselves devoting our time, attention, and efforts more and more to gardening or to painting or to youth groups or to political rallies while our home duties and relationships take second place. Then, because God isn't so obviously urgent, because he doesn't pester us for our attention like our children or a sloppy house can, he, too, may indeed be relegated to the back seat in our lives.

This is why, in the first P, we must consciously include time for God in our schedules, and if we do it first, we can be sure of giving him his rightful place in our lives. He, in turn, will give us the strength and meaning we need to live our vocations.

The Sacrament of Reconciliation

I was back on the road in the following months. I wrote a letter to my mom, apologizing for my waywardness and for what I knew it had done to her. You see, my father had left us when I was seventeen, we had lost our house, and shortly after that, I rebelled and left. It was a rough period for my mother, and I know she cried for a long time. In my letter, I thanked her for *her* integrity, for I can never say that my mother condoned my sin. While she always loved me, she was never afraid to speak the truth. Not for a moment did she hide things under the rug, and she was never afraid to tackle me on my lifestyle if need be.

After setting up the gear at a club one night, I called home to tell Mom I was going to get to Confession that week. The next day at four o'clock, I walked out of the band house. I clutched my rosary and grasped my scapular close to my heart (having selectively re-adopted them from my Catholic upbringing), for I was afraid — not afraid of going to Confession, but afraid of not getting there! I was aware of the radical move I was making, aware that my yes to God was a firm no to the Devil, who might indeed try to stop me. In all honesty, I feared for my life as I walked those three long blocks to the church. While pausing very carefully at intersections to make sure there were no cars coming to run me down, I walked as briskly as I could into the church and entered the confessional for the first time in five years.

A Mother's Rule of Life

I've seen people fearful of Confession. I, too, have had my fears, but in practice, I've experienced in the sacrament only the tremendous outpouring of God's love and grace. Now, that doesn't mean it has always been easy. I remember the time I had to confess a particularly embarrassing sin. I told the priest I didn't want to say it. "You must say it," he replied. So, mustering *all* my courage, I did. My initial flush of shame turned quickly to relief and a real experience of God's mercy as the priest said, "There, you see? It's necessary to confess our sins honestly and openly; it's the only way we can truly confront the horror of what we've done."

But God also knows our weaknesses. He doesn't ask anything of us that we cannot do, or for which he will not provide the necessary grace.

I have found the confessional a wonderful place for counsel and God's solace in my times of struggle. One time in Confession, I relayed my confusion and discouragement to the priest, and he gave me a beautiful analogy that tided me over for the next little while. He compared sin to a ringing bell. "When you're actively sinning," he explained, "it's like you're ringing a bell by its rope, on purpose. Now, after your conversion, you have ceased to pull the rope, but the bell still swings back and forth. But if you listen closely, you'll see that its peals are quieter now, and come further and further apart. Eventually, the ringing will stop altogether. Have patience with yourself, my dear."

In creating a Mother's Rule, we must provide for the means for developing a deeper relationship with God, and the sacrament of Reconciliation is one of the most powerful means we have.

It's true, sometimes we may be scared or reluctant to go, or not having committed any "big" sins, we may see no need to go. But really, Confession is a brilliant invention of God to address our very personal circumstances in a unique and direct way. The graces given in Confession are *specifically targeted* to our most pressing *individualized* needs, both large and small, by a threefold action of God: by forgiving our sin, by healing sinful habits, and by empowering us to live our lives with more grace specially designed for our circumstances.

In addition, when God doesn't seem to be listening to us in any other part of our lives, which can happen quite naturally, his audible voice through the priest is often a great comfort. So we want to ensure in our Mother's Rule that we make use of this sacrament on a regular basis.

The Power of the Eucharist

After my conversion, I spent many months devouring the Word of God after my years-long starvation. Being a traveling musician gave me much free time, and it wasn't unusual for me to be able to spend six hours a day reading the Bible. It was like taking a crash course in Christianity, and the blessings flowed.

In my travels, I met a few Christians here and there, mostly Protestants, and I began to read many Protestant books. I understood that I had had what they term a "born again" experience. And I decided to reject the Catholic Church. Since I had never experienced God "personally" as a Catholic, there seemed no good reason for ever going back. It was the Protestant books that were encouraging me in my walk in the Faith. It was the Protestants who actually talked about Jesus in a normal conversation. It was the Protestants who were on fire for Jesus and who actually lived their lives in a real, living relationship with him. They must be right!

But this concerned my mother. I was home on another break, and Mom cornered me in my room:

"Holly, I want you to get back to Mass."

"I have no intention whatsoever of going back to Mass!" I replied.

"Holly, I want you to get back to Mass," she said again.

I had a reply ready. "I read my Bible six hours a day. How often do you read yours?" I quipped.

"I read my Bible every day at Mass."

"Look, Mom, I'm happy. I love Jesus. I don't want to go to Mass. I don't need Mass."

And this was just the challenge my mother needed. She began to explain to me the importance of the sacrament of the Eucharist.

"Let me put it to you like this, Holly: why would a man, a healthy man who could be very happily married and have his own children, give it all up for a little piece of bread, to offer that little piece of bread, the Eucharist, *unless there was something more to it than bread?*"

I didn't respond, but the thought ran through my head: "Well, I suppose the Holy Spirit could be speaking through her, too."

My mom asked me at least to try. And so I did. The next week I was back in Halifax, and it was Palm Sunday. I found the nearest Catholic church in the phone book and headed over.

From the moment I walked into the church, I could feel the presence of Jesus strongly, and when the priest elevated the host, I knew it was he. I cried all through that Mass. I was quite a sight in my leather jacket, dark shades, and dyed-blond rock-and-roll hairstyle, bawling like a baby, with little children turning around and pointing at me. I cried all through that Mass, and the Mass the next week, and the Mass the next week, and the Mass the next week. For six straight weeks, the moment I walked into the church, I would begin to cry, until finally, I said to Jesus, "Okay, I guess you've convinced me! I'll come back to the Catholic Church!" And *at that very moment*, the tears stopped and never returned.

I love my Protestant Christian brothers and sisters. I see in them a dedication to and seriousness about their faith that's often missing in Catholic parishes. I believe, as a Catholic, I have much to learn from them. I'm inspired by their dedication to the Scriptures, their ongoing study of God's revelation, and their conscious dedication to live according to Christian truth.

But I've come to understand that the Catholic Church contains the *fullness* of that truth. I saw hints of this when I first started coming back to God. I had to relearn everything by serious study and meditation and would often find myself questioning my Protestant friends: "How can you say you're saved and still sleep with your girlfriend?" "If I've been saved because I'm born again, why did my parents bother to baptize me?" "If all I have to look forward to is Heaven to get to God, why did God bother to create me here on earth? Why didn't he just create me right in Heaven?" I asked them these and many other questions in my desire to understand my newfound faith, and over and over again, their reply would be a blank face and a "Gee, I don't really know, Holly." But as a Catholic, I finally found the answers to all the questions I had. I could draw upon the writings and wisdom of Church teaching and popes and saints throughout history, and soon realized I would *never* exhaust the wisdom of Catholicism in my lifetime.

In our Mother's Rule, we need to include some time for study and spiritual reading, for God has a lot to say to us about the vocation he has called us to. But beyond study, there's even more.

Most important, it's the sacraments that most clearly reflect God's intent for us. I can study all I want, but that doesn't mean I can *do* it all. I once said to Philip, "You know, if I really *did* all the things that I've learned from the books I have in my own house, I'd be a saint." For study isn't enough; we need power. That power is found in the sacraments, and most especially in the Eucharist.

As food is for our bodies, so the Eucharistic Bread is for our souls, and our souls house our will, the essential place in our hearts where decisions are made. As study enlightens our mind, the sacraments strengthen our will. Without God's supernatural power in our wills, we'll be too weak to do his will. We can't get to Heaven on our own efforts, nor even perform moral or virtuous acts without his grace. Even our child-raising is dependent upon grace. If we don't set aside time in our Rule for regular reception of the Eucharist, we'll be seriously lacking in the strength to do what we're called to do.

But you know, this doesn't necessarily mean we'll always "feel" it or experience this power consciously. Most of the time, I don't perceive it myself, but I do know that the effects of grace are often perceptible to others — in kindness, in our acts of charity, sometimes even in our physical demeanor. When I had come off the road and was working as a cashier, I came to work one afternoon right after church. One of the waitresses approached me and said, "You've just come from Mass, haven't you?"

"Yeah," I replied.

"I thought so," she said. "I can always tell when you've just gone to church. You're like two different people."

A Dark Night of the Soul

Soon, I sensed God was calling me to leave the music business to return home and attend university. I didn't want to leave. I loved the boys in my band. They were like brothers to me. And besides which, I wanted to be a star.

But God will have his way, and not wanting to refuse him, I told him he'd have to take care of it. "If you want me to leave the band, you'll have to bring it about, for I don't have the strength to do it myself." Within five weeks of uttering this prayer, five separate members of the band, one by one, week by week, were given more lucrative job offers in other bands, and it was only the bass player and I left.

"Okay, okay. I'll go back home!" And I did. I was launched back into a society I had rejected. So many years away, living however I liked, did not prepare me for having to live according to someone else's norms. I had to stay with my aunt and mom because I had no money for an apartment, and there were house rules. I was used to staying up all night, but these people were awake during the day! I got a job as a cashier at a local restaurant, where the manager, having received complaints from some conservative customers, informed me that my wild hair had to be tied up in a bun and my hot-pink jumpsuit had to go, replaced with a dress that went all the way down to the knees! I found myself wiping ketchup goo off highchairs, cleaning tables that someone else had made a mess of, and listening to customers complain about cold coffee. As silly as it might sound, I experienced a real culture shock, and it made my heart sink.

Entering university was good, but my heart didn't seem to recover. I felt my love of Jesus go cold. I had no conscious experience of his presence. After two years, I felt as if I had been picked up, dropped off, and left to fend for myself. I was in such a foreign-feeling situation, I didn't seem to have anything I could count on as real. Depression set in, and Christianity seemed to become, once more, a series of "thou shalts" — a set of rules and regulations.

My prayer life became dry and dismal. Oh, how I hated to have my studies interrupted by my mother, inviting me to pray the evening Rosary. Rebellion would stir in my soul every single night, and I couldn't see how agitated prayer was any good. My mother would say, "Holly, it doesn't matter how you *feel* about it. Just do it. Sometimes the best prayer is the one you don't seem to get much good out of." And so I would bite my lip, mumble my prayers, and ask God to make this count for *something*.

Yes, the time after my conversion was difficult. I just felt bad, and I didn't know where Jesus was anymore. Why had he gone away?

It was at university that I learned of John of the Cross and the Dark Night of the Soul. There I found an explanation of what had just happened to me. What happens when we throw a log on the fire? he asked. The bark begins to get warm, it smokes a bit, and then the bark catches fire in a big way — lots of noise and heat and light. So, too, with me, when I first came to the Lord, the fire of his love set *me* on fire! This is the initial conversion, where we burn with desire for God, and it's very obvious to us and to others. We can't stop talking about God and what he has done for us. This is what Protestants mean by the "born again" experience.

Of course, there are people who can say they've never had this initial conversion, yet live lives close to Jesus. I think this is because, the bigger the sinner, the bigger the conversion experience. It took a very drastic action on the part of God to impress upon me the need to change. I know he coddled me at first in preparation for what was to come, for all the disorders and impurities of my soul to be righted. Like the prodigal son, I needed a big feast to be assured of the Father's love. The other son, the steady faithful one, was jealous of the big feast, but didn't have to be. For those who have been faithful from the beginning, all that the Father has is theirs anyway! They don't need signs and wonders to believe or love God; and there's much merit in this.

But why did that initial fire die? I went and examined a log in my wood stove. What St. John of the Cross said was right: when the bark of a log has almost burned off, the strangest thing happens. It looks as if the fire has gone out. There's no light coming from the log itself. It looks black and charred, oozing water and sizzling. The fire is there, but it has *penetrated* into the interior of the log and can't be seen on the outside. So, too, after our initial conversion, the fire of God's love seems to fade on the outside, and we wonder whether God loves us or whether we love God still. All we see are our own sinful habits, which is the water oozing out of the log. All we see is the blackness and hopelessness because we can't find the fire of God. All we hear is the sizzling of our own complaints. And so I understood that God penetrates deep into our spirits to do his work, secretly, so we can't interfere. When, at times, all seemed to be darkness, I often recalled something Holocaust survivor Corrie ten Boom said: "God is so close, you can only see his shadow."

So I realized that the reality of God's presence was not to be measured by feeling pleasant emotions. It was here I learned that love is composed of *both pleasure and pain,* that God's love *can* be experienced as a darkness, a negative thing, similar to the painful measures a doctor must take to remove a cancerous growth. God had to step in and withdraw me from all that was harming me — sinful actions and sinful desires.

This understanding enabled me to accept internal pain as something of positive value. I also knew, from John of the Cross, that there would come a time, in the future, where the log would begin to change and glow from within, where it would progressively turn into a red glowing ember, and that there would come a time when I would *feel* God's love once more.

A Relationship with God

Meanwhile, I had to ask myself, "What am I supposed to do now? Am I to sit here in desolation while I wait for God to clean me out? Surely there must be something I can *do!*" My university theology professor, Fr. Tom Daley (or FTD, as we affectionately called him) enlightened me as to what a relationship with God consists of. He answered the question of what I could *do*.

"Let me tell you a little story about Johnny and Suzie," he began.

"Johnny and Suzie begin to date. Johnny really likes Suzie, but she, knowing about Johnny's past, says, 'There's only one rule I have to give you: if you want to be with me, you can't see anyone else.' Well, Johnny, just having gotten to know her a little bit, isn't sure about this, but he agrees, because he really does think she's great. From time to time, Johnny sees other girls he might like to go out with, and sometimes he gets secretly mad and resentful toward Suzie, because it seems as if she's cramping his style. But since he does like her, he avoids other women, because if he doesn't, Suzie will break up with him.

"Eventually, though, Johnny realizes there has been a change. Now he finds that he doesn't really *want* to go out with other women anymore. He has truly fallen in love with Suzie and wants to marry her. The external rule that Suzie had imposed has now been transformed into an internal rule from Johnny's heart. Now he is faithful because he loves her.

"And so, for us," continued FTD, "we must realize that *law precedes love*. The laws that God imposes on us from the outside are meant to discipline us, to help our hearts grow into the laws of love which motivate us from within."

So what was I to do? I was to *obey*.

Twofold Obedience

But obedience to God has a twofold nature. The first thing was to obey God in his commands, by avoiding sin and following all the moral norms of the Church. So I studied morality to align my behavior with what God asked. Only later, when the tug toward sin diminished, did I discover a new way to obey: by practicing the virtues and striving to imitate Jesus consciously.

I once read something that compared God to an employer. An employer doesn't usually hire someone for what he *doesn't* do, but in order to fulfill a job. So, too, our Christian calling isn't really only about avoiding sin, but about taking positive steps forward to complete the mission God has entrusted to us. FTD also told us about "freedom from" and "freedom to." He said that God wants us to be free *from* sin, and then to be free *to* work toward all that God intended us to be. My Mother's Rule of Life, then, was this second aspect: obedience to God's will by using my freedom to work toward my vocation, my mission on earth.

∾

Armed with this new, richer understanding of God's law and love, and how obedience to the first helps us to experience the second, I set about trying to make my Mother's Rule reflect that understanding. When I first began, I had two very basic requirements for my Rule: it had to be reasonable, and it had to be practical. Spending hours a day in prayer might seem fine, but not if it conflicts with suppertime!

I had to discern what I believed a basic Christian prayer life would entail. I believed I ought to do my formal prayers, such as my morning offering, every day. I thought a Rosary was necessary. I wanted to spend time with Scripture and also time in quiet reflection and spiritual reading.

But as a busy mom, I also had to figure out how to do all this with little children running around. The only way was to identify the natural lulls I had in my day: times when the children were asleep, when they rested, or when they played outside.

So, given my family's fairly active lifestyle, I decided upon early morning, before the children were up, for my formal prayers and Scripture reading. I assumed I could get half an hour there, and Philip helped me teach the children that they were not to come downstairs until Mummy called them. This took a good long while, I might add. I also made sure they had books and toys in their bedrooms to keep them occupied should they wake up early, and I brought the baby with me for her bottle.

During the morning, the children would often go outside for a little while, so I scheduled an official recess and placed a chaplet or some psalms in that time spot. After lunch, I usually sent the children upstairs for a nap or quiet time, so I arranged half an hour of prayer and spiritual reading there. And I instituted a formal family prayer time in the evening at 7:30, just before the children's bedtime. In the evening, I could do my spiritual reading freely.

But I also was intrigued by the notion of making my whole day a prayer, and so, after each of the time slots I had chosen for prayer, I would try consciously to offer the next chunk of time to God. This helped me maintain recollection, at least for a little while. This conscious awareness of God was the most important thing to me, and so I actually wrote down my prayer schedule on paper and charts so I could just "obey" what was written and free my mind and heart to speak with God throughout my day.

Aside from the daily prayers, there were other things I wanted to ensure: regular Confession, spiritual direction, and Adoration. And I wanted to maintain my Mother's Sabbath, a regular day out every two weeks for rest, solitude, and restoration with God, which I had arranged with Philip a couple of years back. So I went to my calendar and marked off for the next few months what I wanted to see done in these areas.

The First P: Prayer

Working Out Your Essentials

Here I want to get you running as quickly as possible with a basic and essential prayer schedule. For your own sake, keep it simple and easy, at least initially. You'll have time to spice it up and add more later on, when you've gotten used to a basic Rule. To do too much too soon might discourage you and tempt you to give it up. But you *can* do it because God has promised you all the graces you need in your marital sacrament.

Before you begin developing your own Rule, you'll have to get a sturdy notebook or a binder with looseleaf paper. In the following chapters, I'll give you questions to ask yourself that will help you form your own, individualized Mother's Rule of Life.

Be diligent and thorough. If you write down all your responses, plans, and reflections as you go, they will be recorded for future reference, and you'll never need to rethink these things again. All that detail will leave your head and free your mind. And by keeping every idea in one book, you won't have your Rule notes scattered all over the house. You might also want to work in pencil, so you can alter things if you find schedule contradictions.

In my binder, I have a separate page for prayer practices and study projects for the coming year, and another page for the faith life of my children. I have a page specifically for breakfast and morning chores, one for afternoon chores, one for supper chores, and one for bedtime chores. I have a page set aside for each room in my house, and a separate page for each of the following: monthly tasks, weekly routines, Christmas and Easter activities, seasonal chores, gardens, clothing needs, birthday gifts, hobby ideas, and more. This gives you an idea of what may eventually be in your book.

Now, get your Mother's Rule notebook, and set up your first page: "Prayer." Read through and answer the following questions.

Try not to leave a question before you've decided what you're going to do and have written in down. The key to success is to make your Mother's Rule reasonable. It doesn't matter whether you really want to spend huge chunks or little chunks of time in prayer. What counts is that you think it out. Ask yourself:

* *What types of prayer practices do I think are reasonable for any Christian to do on a daily basis?*

* *What limitations or special circumstances do I or my family have?* Consider your personality and tendencies, as well as your family situation. If you're not a morning person, for example, don't schedule in excessively early rising and long morning prayer.

 Do my children interrupt what prayer I do now? If so, how can I help prevent this? Can my husband or older children help me out?

 When are there natural lulls in my day when I could arrange for the children to be occupied in a safe and healthful way so that I can pray?

 Decide upon some basic time slots, no matter how short, to set aside for prayer.

* *Which prayer practices do I want to schedule in which time slots? Which time slots do I want to leave free to choose a form of prayer spontaneously?*

 Decide, and write everything down in your notebook.

* *Is there someplace I can pray without distraction? Where? Can I create a prayer spot, with easy access to my Bible, Rosary, Catechism, and other prayer aids? How about a statue, pictures, and candles?*

 Decide, write down your ideas, and sometime today or tomorrow, set it up.

* *How often do I think is reasonable to get to Confession? When can I do this? Will I take the children with me? If not, who will care for them?*

Could regular Confession conflict with any ongoing commitments? If so, how can I reconcile them?

Decide these things, set up your next three months' Confession times, and write them down.

How often can I get to Mass? What about the children?

What about spiritual direction?

Now, beginning immediately with your next scheduled prayer sessions, drop everything else, and just start praying!

Now you can go over these questions with each of your younger children, or in consultation with your older children, and help them work out basic essential faith practices as well. Use a separate page in your notebook, entitled Children's Prayer Life (or better yet, let them begin their own Rule notebook!), and include family prayer. Encourage them to begin right away as well.

Beyond the Basics

Once you have the basic elements of the five Ps accounted for in your Rule, you may want to look into ways you can go deeper, further refining and enriching the way you live out your vocation.

In the areas of prayer and spirituality, there are other opportunities that might arise given your particular circumstances: prayer groups, Adoration, retreat days, study groups, and personal study. After you've worked through the basics I mentioned and have established a nice, simple prayer schedule, look at the little extras that you might want to do. It may take you a year or more to feel comfortable enough to add them; it will depend on your unique personality and circumstances. But remember, God knows you and what you can handle. He will honor any attempts you make.

Also here you may want to find regular time to reflect on the heart of the first P: your relationship with God. Are there any areas of your life that need more reflection? Are there any habits of sin that you need to examine and seek help to overcome? You could set aside a page in your notebook or a private journal that lists situations or personal habits you'd like to begin dealing with. By keeping track in a conscious fashion, you can decide the means of attack as you go.

Do you need to learn more about God and your Faith? One of our main purposes on earth is to know God. We do this by studying Scripture and the *Catechism*, by reading saints' lives and books on spirituality. What study projects do you need to decide on for the coming year?

Are there any areas of your life that are distracting you from your vocation, especially your time with God? Are you involved in too many things that leave little time for prayer? What can you eliminate, and when will you do this?

Do you feel God calling you to a deeper relationship with him? What do you think he's asking of you? Do you feel you have a relationship with him? What's preventing you from deepening that relationship? Do you need to seek counsel from a priest?

⁀

The purpose of the first P is to bring you closer to God. By consciously setting aside time, and with a firm resolution to follow through, you'll have already made a tremendous movement toward intimacy with him. To foster a growing awareness of his presence in your life, whenever you refer to your schedule or have a spare moment, lift your heart in a little prayer to him asking for His blessing or help with the coming hour. This will supernaturalize your entire day, and eventually, when it becomes a habit, it will sanctify your entire life. And not only that, God *will* come.

Chapter 4

⁀

The Second P: Person

God has given each of us a great gift: the gift of ourselves. We perhaps aren't accustomed to thinking of ourselves that way, yet it's true; our unique person is a special present to us from God. He wants us to be holy, happy, and healthy, and in order to be so, we need to *know* ourselves — our good points and our bad points, our talents and strengths, our weaknesses and our failings. When we truly know ourselves, when we see ourselves with God's eyes, we can become what God intends us to be. And living in conformity with God's intent is the truest path to personal health.

Personal Disintegration

I didn't feel very much like a gift to myself in the months following my conversion. I remember one night, lying on my bed, eyes staring blindly at the ceiling. My mother entered the room and sat down on the bed beside me. Picking up my arm and giving it a little rub, she asked me what was wrong.

"I just feel horrible all the time, Mom. I can't figure out how to stop it." We talked for about half an hour. I shared with her what was going on with me.

I was a mess, and I knew it. I was terribly, desperately unhappy. I just felt bad all the time, and my mind was always clouded and confused. I called it depression, but it was so much more — so undefinable. I wanted to run away and escape, but I didn't know what from. "If I could just crawl under a rock for a couple of weeks, it would be great," I'd think to myself.

On the outside, to all observers at university, I was doing well. I enjoyed the classes, and thoroughly enjoyed the discussions at the round table in the cafeteria. I was getting good marks, and I appeared even to be happy. I seemed so happy that one of my very best friends wouldn't believe me when I told her I was depressed!

I didn't want to feel bad, so I'd try to forget it. Maybe if I just didn't think about things, all my problems would go away. It was easy to pretend there was nothing wrong when I kept myself so busy that I couldn't think about what was going on inside me. As long as I had an interesting paper to write or a social event to pass my time, I was okay. But every night, I had to return to the quiet of my bedroom, and all the despair and depression were still there.

When we don't understand what's going on inside us, it's natural to seek relief from our problems in distraction, but distraction is an escape. As with physical pain, trying to hide from or ignore inner pain never makes it better. My inner pain was an indication of disorder within my person, and I needed to treat this disorder, not just the symptoms. What was going on inside of me? How could I change? How could I be holy and happy and healthy?

What Is a Human?

I began to look for answers to these questions and discovered some interesting and important things about God's intent for me as a person. I learned that human beings are a unique bridge between the spiritual and material orders of creation — a type of composite being, made up of body and soul, interconnected and inseparable.

The Second P: Person

While we share many things with animals, like a physical body, instincts, and the senses, we also share the angelic life; we possess a soul, which is a spiritual reality. In this, we are made in the image of God, who is spirit.

Our souls possess the powers of intelligence and will: our ability to know and think, and our ability to choose. And in the center of our souls is a secret place called the "heart." It's the seat of our emotions and the truest part of our personality. Very closely connected to the will, it's the very core of our being and the place where we essentially decide to live life for God or for self.[8] *Our heart is where God lives. Our heart is where we love.*

God's Intent for Our Person

God's original intent for us was reflected in the gift of integrity given to Adam and Eve at creation. Integrity meant that all the various "parts" of their persons functioned in proper harmony and balance. Adam and Eve were in union with God in their hearts;[9] their intellects informed their wills about what was objectively good, and their wills, attracted to good and strengthened by grace, freely chose it. With these higher faculties functioning smoothly, their emotions were a life-enhancing gift from God, a powerful and positive force to assist in carrying out their decisions.

Adam would never have slept in when there was work to do, and Eve would never have avoided her housework because she didn't feel like doing it. Everything they did was reasonable; they always

---

[8] CCC, no. 368.

[9] Rev. Adolphe Tanquerey, SS, DD. *The Spiritual Life: A Treatise on Ascetical and Mystical Theology*, trans. Rev. Herman Branderis, SS, DD (Tournai, Belgium: Society of St. John the Evangelist, Desclée and Co. Publishers, c. 1930).

chose the good with their wills, and their hearts always wanted to do good. Thus, they were fully living in grace, experienced God's abiding presence deep within their hearts, and were at peace. They were happy. This is God's intent for us as persons, too.

Sin Scatters Our Persons

Adam and Eve, having freely given first place to themselves in their hearts, and permitting their own desires to have unlawful precedence over the command of God, in turn destroyed the proper control of their reason and will over their appetites, and thus began an internal warring of the various human parts, one against the other. This action had a direct effect on us; we, too, experience an interior scattering and a disintegration of the internal order and personal unity originally intended by God. This is called "concupiscence."[10]

We feel it every time our emotions cringe in fear and disgust in reaction to something we know is a good, such as cleaning the attic! We experience it every time we want to eat too many sweets, or sleep too late, or when we want to engage in sinful activities. Instead of subordinating our drives and desires to choose objective good, our wills, damaged and weakened, follow along behind the passions. We tend to choose something that will make us *feel* good, but that might be, in reality, very harmful to us. Our reasoning power is damaged also, and so even grasping truth becomes more difficult than God intended. This leaves our wills uninformed, weakening our decision-making capacities. Our hearts, no longer in line with God's will, seek a selfish fulfillment, and our emotions become a powerful force that can now work against our better reason.

[10] CCC, no. 2515.

The Second P: Person

Counteracting Sin's Effect on Our Persons

I began to realize that not only had I inherited this personal disorder with Original Sin, but I had also seriously aggravated it by my own sinful actions. Every time I chose to sin, I was furthering the scattering process. By rejecting God's grace in my heart, I was fostering the control of my passions over my soul. I was weakening my own will and darkening my own reasoning.

It's important for us in the second P, Person, to realize this is true for all of us. *Our spiritual health directly affects our personal health.* If we want to achieve personal balance, we must recognize the importance of our relationship with God in re-establishing order. Part of what we suffer with the mix-up of our persons is a natural consequence of our own actions, but there are remedies.

First, it requires a serious commitment to adhere to the moral norms God has revealed to us. He has given them to us for our own good — not just an eternal good, but for our health and happiness on earth as well.

Second, we need to take advantage regularly of Confession, for there's a special property of this grace that actually heals the damage we've done to ourselves through sin. Prayer also helps with personal integration.

And third, we must study our Faith, because our intellect can't inform our will about a "good" it doesn't even know about. Such study to help our will make good choices is known as the "formation of conscience."

Psychological and Emotional Health

So I tried to improve my moral life gradually, studied to learn God's principles on which to base my life, and frequented Confession. But my emotional turmoil continued, and I began to realize there was more to personal health than just the spiritual aspect.

My depression was a sign that there was something else going on inside me that I had to address.

Where to start? Initially, I read a few good books on depression. I also consulted a psychologist and a psychiatrist, recognizing the need for professional advice.

Then I began to analyze my life. I tried to step back from any given situation I was in and figure out why I was reacting the way I was. I'd ask myself: Why do I feel this way? Why is this bothering me? Where have I encountered this before in my life? What does this make me think of? This is part of the process of coming to know yourself.

I knew that our bodies are intricately linked with our spirits and that there could be physiological reasons for what I was going through. So, I talked with a number of doctors, inquiring into the possibility of an underlying medical condition that might be caus-ing my difficulties. Many years later, I actually found a dietary cause that affected my moods somewhat. And being a mother up late at night with crying babies revealed very clearly the impor-tance of adequate sleep and rest! Exercise, too, plays an important role in mood control, as doctors are now pointing out. So attend-ing to our physical health also affects our psychological and emo-tional health.

I sought to work out problems in past relationships. There had been people in my life who had hurt me, disappointed me, or whom I felt had rejected me. I tried to come up with other possible expla-nations for their behavior, instead of assuming the worst motives on their part. I discussed certain situations with certain people to help me understand their viewpoint. But most important, I learned to forgive them for any wrongs they had committed against me.

The second P, then, calls for us to take stock of what's going on inside us and seek solutions to any personal problems we have.

There are so many reasons we may have emotional or psychological difficulties; we all have our own unique issues according to temperament, physiology, and personal history. There are so many ways we can and must address this priority in our lives: through study, counsel and self-analysis, nutrition, exercise and rest, and even medication if necessary. *We need to do what we can*, and look at all the various areas because *our psychological and emotional health is essential* to the fulfillment of our vocation. We can't give to others what we don't have. We can't minister fully to our families when our eyes are turned inward to pain.

God Wants to Do His Part

Despite working very hard to restore myself to emotional and mental health, years had passed, and I was *still* having difficulties. Sometimes, there would be an undue heaviness about life, almost a blackness at times, that would rise up unexpectedly and incapacitate me. Some days when I got up, I would sit at the kitchen table, unable to get up and do my duties, just feeling overwhelmed by the internal struggle. I could never tell whether I was going to be feeling good or bad, and the drama of it all was wearing on me.

So, I commended myself to the Blessed Mother and asked her to put someone in my path who could help me. I offered it all up to God, as best as I could. And then, one day, God answered my prayer. I ended up in the confessional.

"Father, last week, on Good Friday," I whispered to the priest from behind the grill, "I was doing some spiritual reading, and I found myself scoffing. Scoffing! Now, I have a solid faith, and I don't know where this is coming from."

"What else is going on in your life right now?" he asked.

"My life is a mess!" I told him. "I don't know what I'm suffering from; I guess you could call it depression, yet it's not depression all at the same time. All I can tell you is that I just feel bad, and life seems to be extraordinarily *hard*."

"Have you seen anyone about it?" he asked. I moved from behind the grill into the chair in front of him.

"I've seen and done all I know how. I went to a psychologist, but I explained myself so thoroughly that she began to cry and grabbed a Kleenex. I've gone to psychiatrists, doctors, and even gynecologists, suspecting PMS. I've given up eating sugar, drinking coffee, and smoking, and when nothing changed, I started them all again. I've seen priests too — one who was suffering just as much as I was and could offer no solution, and another who calmly walked me to the door and told me there was no one east of Ottawa who could help me! I've analyzed my life until I was blue in the face, prayed novena after novena, and studied everything I can get my hands on, and still, these bad feelings never completely go away. So, have I seen anyone; have I done anything? Yes, I have."

He was silent for a long moment. "Well . . ." he pondered in silence again. Then he said finally, "God doesn't want you to live like this."

"What?" I replied, shocked. I told him I had been offering it up as a cross for years.

"This is no cross," he said. "God wants to heal you, and I'm going to stick by you until he does!" And with that, he got up from the chair, came and laid his hands on my head, and prayed in a silent, searching way.

I felt a warmth spread through my entire body; afterward, I couldn't remember anything else he said during that time except to call him for an appointment. I left the confessional with hope, for the first time in years, that there was something that could actually be done for all the moods and personal struggles I had gone through. But what struck me the most was that he said he would stick by me until I was better. No one had ever said that before, and I was deeply moved.

The Healing Power of God

I went back to see this priest. As I drove to the appointment, I began to feel sick, but nothing was going to stop me from finding the solution to my problems! As soon as I entered his office, the nausea completely left. We talked about my past and upbringing. The priest told me he was going to lead me through some healing prayer, a healing of memories. He was just going to pray over me and lay his hands on me.

"Sure," I said, and he began.

He walked me through all the important scenes of my life, and all the significant people I had known and prayed for. Again I began to feel heat flow through my body, and I began to realize this wasn't some hormonal hot flash, but the presence of the Holy Spirit.

On the way home, the strangest thing happened. I started to see events from my life pictured in my head, as if they were on TV. And they started to fly by, scene by scene, so rapidly, that it became a second-by-second flash film of everything that had ever happened to me. I felt God's presence so strongly, and I arrived home amazed.

All that night, and well into the next day, I felt a powerful sense of relief come over me. Just like a pressure cooker when the top has been opened, letting the steam come out in little spurts, I sighed, and sighed, and sighed, and sighed — over and over again. I felt a weight being lifted off my chest and being replaced with an interior "lightness" I had never felt before. At one point, I just stood in the kitchen and said to Philip, "I can't stop sighing!"

And I came to realize that God had done something very special to me — "spiritual surgery," I called it. When I had done all in my power and had come up against a brick wall, the Divine Physician had come himself and healed me of all the hurts, the memories, even the things I hadn't consciously remembered until now. It struck me that God had been with me in all those events and relationships, and that he had loved me through each of them, even when others didn't seem to. I was consoled that God loved *me*, that he understood my pain, and that he *wanted* to help me.

God wants us to help ourselves, to do what we can through our own efforts to achieve personal wholeness. He wants us to take advantage of the normal means to access grace he has already provided through prayer and the sacraments and study. He also wants to help us through indirect means — the work of professionals and the counsel of family and friends. But I believe that he also wants to intervene directly if these other methods fail to bring complete relief. In the absence of any other hope, God has been known to do the miraculous. And I don't think it's presumptuous to ask him for that.

We can learn to recognize the signs of needing God's direct healing. I myself found that if certain memories of events from even twenty years ago could still make my stomach turn or cause tears to flood my eyes, that was an indication that I needed God's extraordinary intervention. Pains that didn't go away, no matter how much I wanted them to, or how much I analyzed or understood them or sought counsel, were also an indication. For really, these weren't just scars; memories of experiences that are still fresh with emotion are in reality open wounds.

This kind of pain can be contrasted with God's purifying action in our souls, the dark nights, which can also cause "bad" feelings. But these are different. Such actions of God are not necessarily connected to any specific event or memory. They're often interspersed with consoling experiences of God and moments of peace. Often, one can notice a change in oneself and that progress is being made in aligning oneself to God's will. *Purifying* pain brings with it the grace to accept it, and to give oneself trustingly, offering oneself to the Father with Jesus. Pain in need of healing brings despair and discouragement.

Spiritual Warfare and Deliverance

Two weeks later, I was back at the priest's office. "Something's not right," he said. "You've done everything you can do, from doctors to psychologists, Confession, the healing of memories, the Sacrament of the Sick. . . . I think you might need deliverance."

"Deliverance?" I asked, perplexed.

"Deliverance from demonic harassment. Somewhere in your life, you have opened a door, and the Devil walked in."

Could this be so? It was true: way back when I was nine years old, I had begun to have a fascination with the occult. I read books on all sorts of occult topics: poltergeists, astrology, ghosts and spirit worlds, palm reading, voodoo. I had dabbled with a Ouija board, and played "séance" as a kid with my friends. This had led to a deeper involvement with the occult that ended only after one extremely frightening personal experience of the demonic world when I was seventeen. It was so horrible and threatening, I threw out everything I owned that dealt with the occult, and I had never ever watched, read, or allowed near me anything to do with the occult again. I mistakenly thought that was the end of it all.

Nonetheless, the priest sent me to see another priest who dealt with that kind of thing.

"You see, there are a number of things the Devil can do to us," he said to me. "First, on one end of the spectrum, he can tempt us;

this is something he can do with everyone. This happens without our permission. On the other extreme end of the spectrum, he can possess someone. This usually only happens when he has been invited to."

In the middle, he said, there was something called "obsession." People open themselves to being obsessed usually by one of three ways: by promiscuity, by drug abuse, or by dabbling in the occult.

"Emotional turmoil is a clear sign of obsession," he continued. "With obsession, the Devil rides your emotions like a wild stallion. One minute you're flying high, and the next five hours you're in the depths of Hell. The next day, everything is wonderful, and then for weeks, you can't escape the gloom. He usually hides himself behind other conditions to evade your notice. PMS is a good one; depression is another. But the normal means of dealing with these things don't work."

We booked a deliverance prayer session for that evening. We began with a period of discernment by the priest and a nun with whom he worked, with my husband, friend, and the first priest all there praying. I was called to "bind, rebuke, and cast out" any demons who were harassing me, one by one, by name — the names corresponding to what the demons do. It was important that *I* be the one to do it, to reject them verbally, for I had invited the unwelcome activity of the Devil by my own behavior.

I believe there can be no complete freedom in this area without the intervention of a holy priest. The importance of the priest can't be undervalued; some graces are simply not available except through him. This is God's choice, and we have to accept that.

The Necessity of Spiritual Direction

These experiences point to the need to include in our Rule time for obtaining and meeting with a spiritual director on a regular basis. So often we can't discern what's going on inside us without the help of an outside, faith-based perspective. Our disordered human nature, sin, psychological and emotional wounds, painful memories, demonic interference, and even God's purifying work can all cause confusion. We need a director to help us discern and set a path for us to follow.

But one of the conditions of the success of such counsel is that we commit to complete and detailed honesty with the confessor and spiritual director. A priest is usually not a mind-reader; he needs to be shown the whole picture. To hide things or omit even seemingly unimportant details can block the full operation of grace. What might seem minimal to us may be the keystone of the whole issue.

Spiritual and personal freedom also calls for a wholehearted decision on our part to do what we're told to do. What my director tells me is not an option, but a real direction from God, as my director stands in God's place. We must learn to obey.

Seeking Christian Freedom

After the healing and deliverance sessions, my emotional heaviness was greatly relieved. I felt as if I had a new lease on life, and everything became easier. Yet despite all the remedies I had undertaken in my own life to achieve personal balance, and despite all the perhaps extraordinary interventions of God I had experienced, I still had one little problem.

That problem was a nasty little personal motto that had followed me all my life: "But I don't *want* to!" Of all the difficulties I had encountered in my search for personal wholeness, perhaps my greatest enemy was my interior spirit of rebellion. My reluctance to let go of my own will and my resistance to doing what I was supposed to do instead of what I *wanted* to do were preventing me from moving closer to God and to happiness.

What was I to do? I remembered something Fr. Tom Daley, my university professor, had said about freedom: "Freedom is taking responsibility for who you are to become." Now, that was *not* a familiar concept. Our society's idea of freedom, and the one I had functioned with for so long, meant the "right" to do whatever I wanted, free from external restraint. But I had to ask myself, "Is doing what I want, even if it hurts me, really freedom? And when I find it so hard to do what's best for me, can I honestly say I'm free?"

True freedom, then, Christian freedom, is when *we willingly take the steps needed to return ourselves to the internal order God intended.* Only then can we experience God, who lives in our center.

> [This freedom] is not innate but acquired; not a product of nature but of nurture; something that must be won over and over again; a . . . struggle against the appetites, inclinations, instincts and passions which threaten to enslave the individual. . . . [It means] an interior submission to the voice of the Spirit, devotion to duty, loyalty to one's word, staunch adherence to principles, fidelity to conscience and trust in God. . . . [These are] the guarantees of genuine liberty. To serve God is to rule.[11]

So we are all called to Christian freedom — to take responsibility for the person God intends us to become. Thus, there has to come a time when we begin consciously to act in conformity with what we know to be good. This means engaging the will. I reached a point where I realized I had to stop so much reading and begin *doing*. To make a straight path to God in my heart, I had to train

---

[11] Rev. Franz de Hovre, Ph.D., *Catholicism in Education*, trans. Rev. Edward B. Jordan, MA, St.D. (New York: Benzinger Brothers, 1934.)

myself to do what is right. Over time, this habit of doing good strengthens the will and helps to tame the other parts of us that may battle each other.

And this is where my terrible little motto came in! At times, following my conscience and doing what God wanted or doing what I believed was best for me or others seemed horrible. Life can seem dry and depressing when you can't get your own way!

Nonetheless, it was primarily up to me to live my life the way I knew I ought to. So many times I wanted to shirk my responsibilities because someone else in my life wasn't acting the way I wanted them to. If God wasn't speaking to me, I wanted to avoid prayer. If my husband was in a grouchy mood, I didn't feel I had to be civil toward him. If my children were noisy or rebellious, I gave myself permission to become impatient.

But if I'm responsible for who I am to become, it doesn't matter whether anyone else in the whole world is doing what I think they ought to do; I'm answerable to God for what I *do*. This is Christian freedom.

It's also the essential Christian struggle. It's the call to imitate Jesus. This is never easy! I recall something Pope John Paul II said at the World Youth Day 2002:

> People are made for happiness. Rightly, then, you thirst for happiness. Christ has the answer to this desire of yours. But he asks that you trust him. True joy is a victory, something which cannot be obtained without a long and difficult struggle. Christ holds the secret of this victory.

And so, for our Rule, we all need to commit to do what we ought to do, and pray to God to convert the very depths of our hearts if necessary. And God *will* work within us to change us, although sometimes it can be painful. But for every crucifixion, there is a resurrection. Order is established. Peace and consolation do come.

Working Our Way Back to Integrity

I was relieved to note that this journey to personal integrity is indeed a *process*, which meant I didn't have to be perfect right away. There was no more pressure to be something I wasn't. I could humbly admit my imperfection as a person, because if God himself wasn't rushing it, I could have patience with my growth as well.

But most profoundly, I discovered another benefit to personal health. Since God lives in the heart, I was not to seek some Being way up in the sky past the clouds; my journey to God was not outward, but inward! The only way to get closer to God was to become ordered enough inside to enable me to experience him within. When our emotions are running loose, and our minds are confused, and our wills are weak and indecisive, and our imagination is working overtime, there's so much internal noise that we can't hear the still voice of God present in the core of our being, our hearts. The disorder in my person made me deaf to him.

⁀

I also discovered that I had unique personal needs that were just as important as any other responsibility I've already mentioned. Aside from all the concerns of my mental and emotional health, and the needs of my body for adequate sleep and exercise and proper nutrition, I also needed to get more quiet time in my life.

So many times over my years as a mother, I had felt tired, overwhelmed, and worn out. So often I felt I couldn't get any personal space to think, what with the continual onslaught of "Mummy! Mummy!" coming from the children, or the work that I hadn't finished staring me in the face. I needed quiet time alone.

I brought my concerns to my spiritual director, and he heartily approved. He said being home all the time afforded me no change and was, in a way, unbalanced. He could easily see how a regular day out would help. He encouraged me to discuss it with my husband.

So, I figured out my game plan and took it to Philip. I told him I needed more space, more time to myself for quiet and reflection, and that I had to have it on a regular basis. I told him about one stay-at-home mom I knew who went out every Saturday while her husband watched the kids. I told Philip that although I would *like* to get out every week, I didn't think that was feasible for our family. After all, he and the kids had needs, too. I decided it would be reasonable for me to go out every *other* Saturday for the day. I reassured him that my spiritual director had supported this and that I was really talking about a personal *need*, not just a want or a desire to escape.

His reaction shocked me a bit. "Well, there's no *other* woman I know who gets a day off every two weeks!" His obstinance wasn't characteristic. A short argument followed, for I felt I had to stand up for what I believed God was asking of me. I was a little hot under the collar, but in the end, Philip agreed to try it, and I apologized for my flare of temper.

I knew Jesus himself took time away from his public ministry to be alone with his Father, and his job was more important than mine. I knew Jesus had called his disciples away from time to time for quiet and reflection. I knew priests got a whole day off each week. Even St. Elizabeth Seton left her children on Sundays to go to Mass and visit friends. I had thought this through, and I knew I was being reasonable. I wasn't out to abuse it.

But Philip had his own concerns, of course. His list of Saturday chores often piled up — repairs, lawn care, car maintenance — and if I left him alone with five children under the age of eight, he knew he wasn't going to get much done. He experienced a combination of feelings, from being trapped to being stymied, because he couldn't get his work done as it was, and now every other Saturday was "gone." He, too, had to come to terms with his own difficulties, and this situation seemed to bring some of them to light.

I told him he could hire a babysitter for the time I was away if he wanted. Philip was a trooper, however, and he truly tried to overcome his reluctance. On Saturday mornings, he would cheerfully say to me, "Go! Come back when you're ready." But then he would struggle. He struggled with it for a year.

On my part, there were many temptations not to go; sometimes things would come up, usually in Philip's schedule, and I'd have to say firmly, "No, that is my Mother's Sabbath." Philip learned to schedule around it. Other times, I left feeling guilty or pressured because I knew Philip was having difficulty with it. But in the end, he admitted that it had been a call to him to deepen his understanding of fatherhood, and that it was a *good* thing I had decided to do this. He's now perfectly happy with being home alone with the kids every two weeks.

Coming home so refreshed and ready to begin again confirmed that I was doing the right thing. I also offered Philip the same courtesy, and so, on alternating Saturdays, he's free to come and go as he pleases. I assume responsibility for the day with the children, even though he usually stays with us anyway. By the time Philip finishes his week at work, he's glad to be home and doesn't have the same need I do to leave the house.

I've seen people shocked by my Mother's Sabbath, and others intrigued. I have seen some women wishing they could do it, too, but feeling that it's really just a "luxury" they can't afford. I guess it boils down to whether there's a need for retreat. Dom Chautard in *The Soul of the Apostolate* says, "A monthly retreat [taking up an

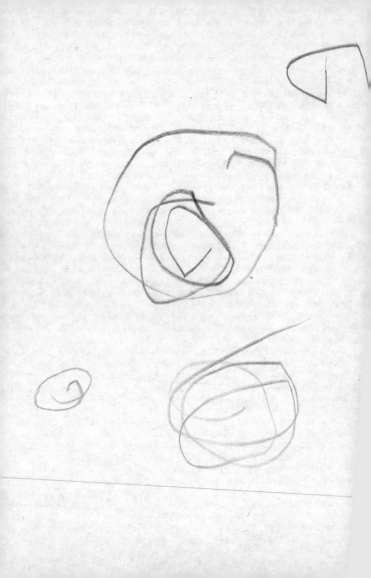

entire day or at least half a day] devoted to a serious effort to recover the equilibrium of the soul is almost indispensable to the active worker." Moms are certainly active workers!

So, I would go out on my Mother's Sabbath, and I'd blast my Christian rock music very loudly all the way to town and sing at the top of my lungs! Then I'd just potter around for a while. I'd go to a favorite bookstore and read the titles for an hour or more. I'd get a lunch somewhere and sit and read, or drive down by the harbor and stare at the sea for a while, writing in my journal or reading a saint's life. Later, I'd head over to Confession and say a Rosary or do some Adoration. Then I'd do any necessary errands I had, although I made sure these were kept to a minimum.

The fruit of all this? I'd come home only when I was ready, and not until I was ready. Sometimes this was three o'clock, normally five or six o'clock, and one time, eleven o'clock! I'd come home refreshed and ready to get on with the next two busy weeks of my mothering business. My children, who took me for granted sometimes, began to greet me at the door as if I'd been away for years, and smothered me with hugs and kisses, so glad to see me.

And so, when you develop your Rule, take into consideration *all* your legitimate needs, and be determined to meet what *must* be met for your own personal health, but always in consultation and negotiation with your family. And remember that sometimes your family might need to sacrifice a little bit for you, too, when it comes to your complete personal health. For as we've already discussed, when you're properly ordered, you can minister to them much more effectively and lovingly.

Working Out Your Essentials

Here, you want to ensure that you're getting what you need — for your body and your spirit. Initially, you want to focus on basics, perhaps just figuring out the time frames when you'll take care of yourself. Because family life is lived in common, much of what you're about to organize will be the same for each member of your family, so you might want to consider that you're doing a family schedule here, too.

Get your notebook, and label the next clean page, "Daily Routines." On a separate page, label it "Children's Daily Routines." Work through the questions for yourself first, and then go back through them to meet your children's needs. Ask yourself:

• *How much time do I sleep every night now? Is this enough, or do I find myself exhausted by midafternoon every day? How much time do I think I reasonably need to add to or subtract from my present sleep habits? Do I need nap times? When can I schedule these?*

Establish a rising hour that gives you ample time to meet your morning responsibilities. Count back from your rising time the number of hours you need to sleep, and you'll have established your bedtime.

Apply all this to the varying ages of your children, too.

Decide, and write it down in your notebook.

• *What are the basic hygiene and grooming tasks I must do every day, and how much time do I need to do them? Can I do them before or after meals to make them part of a larger chore time and thus make them easier to remember? What basic time can I set to do these regularly?*

Repeat this process for the children. *Do any of them need my specific help? If so, how much time do I need to allot to this, and when will I do it?*

Decide when you will do these tasks, and write it down.

• *How can I get my body moving and in shape? What forms of exercise would I like to do more? How much time do I need periodically to do this? Where and when — morning, afternoon, evening, before or after supper?*

Can the children do any of this with me? If not, where will they be, and who will watch them? How will their exercise needs be met?

Write it all down in your notebook. If you're going to do it only once or twice a week, establish which days you want to exercise on. Create a new page in your notebook entitled "Weekly Routines" and enter your information there.

• *How often do I think is reasonable for me to get out with friends? Do I prefer socialization to be regular or spontaneous?*

What hobbies or other forms of recreation do I need to engage in each day to help balance my day and help release stress?

When would there be a natural time for me to do these things? When the kids are in bed? During their nap time? After supper?

Are there any other personal needs unique to me, for which I need special time?

Set a time for each activity, or a general period available for "recreation." Write this information down on either your daily or weekly routines pages. If you need to, create a monthly routines page for monthly activities.

Begin each of these activities now, starting with the very next item on your schedule. Stop everything else in those time frames, and just do it!

Beyond the Basics

There are other things you might want to look at over time regarding your physical needs and those of your family. Perhaps you could research ways to make exercise more fun and thus easier to stick to; study a bit about nutrition and make up meal plans for more-healthful eating; analyze your eating, drinking, and sleeping habits, or any other habits that may not be helping your body perform at top efficiency.

But most important are the aspects of the second P, the heart of your person, that can't be scheduled. Are there personal issues you need to address? Perhaps you could set aside half an hour every evening or every week to look at all the areas of spiritual, mental, and emotional health, and consider ways in which you need to inform your intellect or strengthen your will. Then, look at your options; would any of these things help: Confession, prayer, study, healing, deliverance, counseling, or just plain old decision-making? Consider starting a journal to record personal areas you need to work on.

~

The purpose of the second P is the health of our person, in all its multifaceted aspects. By carefully caring for our physical health, we remove any unnecessary burdens on our spirits. We must also become conscious of what's going on inside us, to be aware of why we're acting and thinking and choosing as we do.

In *The Spiritual Life*, Fr. Tanquerey tells us that without self-knowledge, it becomes morally impossible to perfect ourselves. Because without it, we instead become subject to illusions about ourselves, becoming either presumptuous about our own perfection or excessively discouraged over our faults.

And although such a process can be complex at times, striving for self-knowledge is considered a general means of seeking perfection. The recognition of our good qualities can lead us to gratefulness to God, while our imperfections can bring true humility, where finally *we see ourselves as we truly are*. This, in turn, helps increase our dependence on God and moderates any unrealistic expectations we may have of our abilities, but also firmly motivates us to become all that God intends for us to be.

⇌

Chapter 5

The Third P: Partner

With the third P, Partner, we begin to look at the sacrament of Marriage itself, and specifically to what the *Catechism* refers to when it speaks of marriage as a special type of *consecration*.[12] To consecrate something means to set it apart for a special purpose, and in the third P, we deal with the *first* purpose of the sacrament of Marriage: the development of a deep and personal relationship between the spouses, reflecting the special grace of unity shared by married couples.

And as with Holy Orders, we need to realize that the sacrament of Marriage is meant to enable us to fulfill a *mission* — in this instance, a mission of service and love toward our spouse.

A Reluctant Romance

It was September, my twenty-seventh birthday. As I was preparing to go out for a night on the town with my friends, my mother entered my bedroom, bearing gifts from Philip. I opened the lovely box of chocolates and drank in the scent of the gorgeous long-stemmed roses, but then immediately I could feel my temper rise. Why, how dare he? He knew better than this!

[12] CCC, par. 1535.

Still single, I had just entered a Bachelor of Education program that fall, and Philip had moved away to another university in Ottawa and was doing his master's there. I had told him that if I ever did marry, it would certainly be to him — because he would make a great husband and father — but that I had no intention ever to do so. After all, Philip was my *friend*, and I was going to keep it that way, no matter how I felt about him, because I had sworn off romance forever. I was going to finish my degree and decide whether God was calling me to become a nun.

And now, from halfway across the country, he dared to send me flowers and chocolates! I called him and accused him of a hidden agenda. "You sent me courting gifts! How *could* you send me courting gifts?"

Of course, Philip played innocent and told me he was very sorry; he really hadn't thought about the significance of flowers and chocolates. He just wanted to send a little something to commemorate my birthday, seeing as how we were friends, and was that a sin or something?

Back home during his Christmas break, I was still getting little hints that Philip might be interested in more than friendship. Out at a dinner with him one evening, I accused him of tempting me from my vocation.

"I'm going to be a nun," I said, "and you're setting out to take me away from the vocation God himself is calling me to! Be careful!" But Phil just laughed out loud.

I was puzzled at his casual dismissal and slightly annoyed at the sneaky grin on his face. To me, this was serious business!

Way back on my thirteenth birthday, I had vowed I'd never get married. Even at the tender beginnings of puberty, I felt there were so many more *important* things to devote myself to; why, I could be a rock star or a politician or a lawyer, or have a career in advertising! The world was wide open, and nothing could be less important than getting married, having kids, and painting a little white picket fence!

My resistance to marriage was strongly reinforced when my parents separated after twenty-six years of marriage. At seventeen, I had concluded that marriage was a *bad* thing, a farce, something fraught with tension and misunderstandings that could only end in pain. After watching my mother cry every day for a year, I knew it wasn't for me. I'd never consent to being left so vulnerable and open to such intense feelings of rejection.

But my most fervent renunciation of marriage had come after my conversion, for I could not for the life of me see how I could love Jesus and still love a man. The two seemed mutually exclusive. I saw no correlation between a life of faith and marriage; how the "worldliness" of marriage, with its temporal concerns and responsibilities, could be conducive to holiness or growing closer to the Lord.

A Surprising Call from God

The following spring, Philip returned to my hometown, and I naturally spent time with him, for he was a good friend — in fact, my best friend. But over the summer, I began to sense something new: a call to marriage, and to Phil! In my confusion, I consulted a couple of priests, and they tended to confirm what I was discerning. I went to a nun I knew and told her my dilemma. She gave me good counsel: I was to look into religious life and date Phil simultaneously.

Still feeling unsettled, I decided that autumn to make a pilgrimage for discernment to Ste. Anne de Beaupré, a famous Quebec shrine known for many miraculous cures. I spent two days at the basilica, praying intensely for guidance. At one point, I was praying before a statue of an older saint when I leaned over to see his name. It was St. Joachim. My heart stopped. I looked from his statue to the larger statue of St. Anne in the main church. I glanced back and forth between the two and gasped, "St. Anne was married to St. Joachim!"

My middle name is Anne, and Philip's is Joachim.

Anne and Joachim! Philip and I! I was sure I had received an answer.

But once back home, my uneasiness with the possibility of a married vocation continued to plague me. I just kept praying to God, "If you want me to marry, you'll have to make *me* want it, for I just can't see how marriage has anything to do with me!" And as is customary with the way God works with me, by January, after the typically long period of confusion, there came a moment of re-alization: I saw the words "I love you" pop into my imagination just like a moving neon sign, and I knew at that moment that, yes, I *wanted* to marry Philip. I experienced no further doubts.

Philip and I were married, appropriately, on the feast day of St. Anne and St. Joachim, July 26, that year.

Marriage Is Important

Despite my newfound convictions and my love for Philip, it took me many years to overcome some of the difficulties I had with the married vocation itself. But since I knew God had called me to it, I had to trust that he would provide the graces necessary for a successful marriage. And considering my own background, I also had to trust in Philip's stable upbringing to break any cycle of failure I might be subject to. I also studied and prayed to learn how to have a good marriage.

What helped me the most, however, was my discovery that marriage was an integral part of God's plan for creation in the first

place. "In the beginning . . . he made them male and female. . . ."[13]
When I did a Bible study of the books of Genesis and Exodus, I was
amazed to find that every major figure in these Old Testament
books was married! Adam, Noah, Abraham, Isaac, Jacob, Joseph,
Moses. . . . For goodness' sake, the Blessed Mother was married!
Somehow the mystery of marriage, its mission, and the communion of spousal love were paramount to God's plan. And I came to
understand that having been called to marriage, I would become
holy only through this vocation.

A Serious Disillusionment

Philip and I spent our honeymoon driving across Canada. I was
pregnant before we got to our new home in Calgary, and Philip
and I both got teaching jobs with the local Catholic school board
almost immediately.

Those first two years of marriage saw unexpected difficulties.
The stresses of new careers, a geographical change, few family or
friends around, a first pregnancy with severe sickness and then a
new baby, new financial considerations and being launched into
family responsibilities we were unfamiliar with placed a severe
strain on us. And the way we handled the stress was completely
wrong. We stopped praying together as a couple, and tension and
pressure entered our usually close relationship.

I felt Philip was no longer the man I had married; the loving
and attentive man I'd been engaged to was now preoccupied with
the demands of his new job and aloof toward me. I missed our long
and engaging talks, especially when I had had the baby and was
home on maternity leave. Being so far away from home with few
family or friends, I often felt abandoned, unwanted, and lonely. I

[13] Gen. 1:1, 27.

wanted Philip to spend all his free time with me, to make up for my isolation.

Over time, in my heart, I began to feel that I'd been conned — that marriage really *was* what I'd originally feared it would be. My heart began to close up, and I began to trust Philip less. I grew increasingly unhappy at home and felt rejected by Philip's resistance to talk when he came home from work in the evenings.

Philip on the other hand, didn't want to talk because he felt that I always had a "problem," and he couldn't handle any more problems. To him, my unhappiness was just another stress on his growing list of stresses, and one that he didn't know how to solve. He also helplessly realized that I was interpreting his preoccupation as a rejection, as a diminishment of my importance to him. But with the workload he had, he knew he just couldn't keep up the long leisurely hours of our engagement days, when he had time to rub my feet or play cards.

After all, he had responsibilities now, and he felt hurt by my lack of sympathy to the pressures *he* was feeling in his work. Financial concerns plagued him and undermined his self-confidence, for to him, they were a sign of failure in his mission to provide for his family. He didn't even want to pray with me, because he felt my spiritual life would somehow invade or overshadow his own. What he really wanted was for me to "be there" for him, to support him, but I was too wrapped up in my own struggles.

By the time we moved back to the East Coast, Philip and I were both experiencing a very serious disillusionment about each other, and about all our lofty, idyllic goals of the perfect marriage. Instead, we were growing increasingly alienated, and we weren't getting from each other what we were looking for.

I remember sitting on the edge of the coffee table looking at Philip one night, and he looking at me, and thinking, "This is the point where people get divorced." I wanted to ignore him, forget him, and live my own life away from the responsibilities we shared. Philip just felt hopeless and wanted to escape from the problems.

What a painful and repulsive moment it was. We had no intentions of divorcing, and I wondered whether I couldn't just ignore him and carry on in my own little world. Almost anything seemed better than marriage, and I didn't want to exert the effort to make it better. When Philip finally said, "I suppose we should work this out," my heart actually cringed.

And then we made a *very tiny little decision*, which was about all we could do, given the weakened state of our reluctant and discouraged wills: we decided to attend a six-week Lenten series at our church, one hour a week, as a sign of our commitment to each other and to God. It was the only thing we could see to do that wouldn't overexert or overburden our already burdened spirits.

And *that* decision was the grace of our sacrament in action. Even though we seemed to get little from the content of the talks that Lent, our commitment to work at our marriage resulted in the beginnings of a real change between us.

The Mission of Marital Love

I began slowly to realize that the health of a marriage depends upon our definition of love. When I married Philip, I did so because I "loved" him. But in retrospect, I think my vision of "love" was at least partly selfish in its orientation. I was looking for "the happily ever after" ending of the fairytale. I wanted him to make me feel as pampered and content as I had felt during our engagement. I wanted Philip to support *me*. And I expected that love meant the constant consolation of God mixed in with everything!

But I began to realize that marital love was not what the fairytales said. Love wasn't about emotionalism or sentimentality.

It wasn't erotica or sexual chemistry. It wasn't romance or warm fuzzies or affection. It wasn't even friendship or companionship. I realized marital love was not fundamentally something I was supposed to *seek for myself*.

Instead, I started to see the *mission* inherent in the special consecration of our sacrament. God had given me a job to do, as a wife. Love was something I was supposed to concern myself with giving, not receiving; giving to my husband the *gift of myself*: the gift of my time, my support, my presence, my entire person. So, slowly, I began to offer myself to him, to place myself at the service of his person, to think of his needs above my own, and to marvel at the gift of this wonderful man God had placed in my life. This man who also began to learn to love me, to serve me, to console me — despite all my weaknesses and faults!

This change always begins with God's grace. But as wives, we have to cooperate with grace. This is not always easy. At particularly difficult times, when I simply didn't want to be nice or do something for Philip, I would think I didn't love him at all! But slowly, I began to realize that to give myself to him, to love him, to be there for him, even when I didn't feel like it, was perhaps the greatest love of all.

That's because *real love is a decision, not a feeling*. It's an act of the will, a giving of ourselves to the other for the other's good. This is an ongoing process, not something mastered all at once, and sometimes it can be downright unpleasant, like all crucifixions of selfishness. It doesn't always provide all the emotional rewards we expect, at least not initially.

A Dark Night of the Soul in Marriage

It was here that I realized that the tremendous disillusionment we had gone through was a *dark night of the soul in marriage*. As we are in fact one, unified through the sacrament, our married love is going to be purified and transformed by God. Just as God purges the sinfulness of an individual's soul to foster a relationship with him, so, too, will he do this for those called to a relationship with him as a couple.

St. Faustina assures us that God uses *everything* to effect our transformation — that he wastes not one little trial to bring about a good.

Characteristic of a dark night is a type of blindness — not seeing any evidence that there's something very important going on. In marriage, the reality of our sacramental love is often obscure — something that goes deeper than we can sense or consciously grasp. Just as God's most intense actions in our souls are hidden, purely spiritual, and so not picked up by our intellects or emotions, so, too, the periodic lack of satisfaction in marriage can often lead us to think there's no love.

But the difficulties and dryness of these phases aren't meant to be the end. In God's plan, there's meant to be a resurrection for every crucifixion. When the more selfish love between Philip and me seemed to have died, we began to experience the subtleties of a purer, more selfless love and the realization that to love each other is a primary task of our vocation.

Fulton Sheen once said that it's for this very reason that the marriage vow is in place; the vow is meant to protect the marriage from the natural human desire to leave when things seem to go awry. The vow is meant to be the protection, the chain, that keeps the couple together long enough for God to transform their marriage. As Sheen said, the high divorce rates in our society are not so much a sign that these couples have more serious problems than others, but that they *simply do not keep their word*. Many couples, having insufficient catechesis, misinterpret what's happening in their marriage and erroneously come to believe the marriage has ended. Hence, it seems only logical to get divorced.

And so it gave me hope that, despite the dark times, the times when a loving relationship with my husband seemed impossible, when it all seemed on the verge of collapse, God was indeed working, that he was present whether I saw him or not, and that he was going to pull us through. And he did.

The Necessity of Good Communication

With any sacrament, there are always *words* accompanying the bestowal of grace. The priest pronounces verbally the absolution of Confession with the Sign of the Cross, and the sacrament is effected. So, too, in marriage, we pronounce the vows on our wedding day, and, combined with the consummation of the marital act, they effect the sacrament.

The spoken word is also meant to be a continuing source of grace in marriage, by way of an ongoing, healthy communication with our spouse. Communication is a channel for grace to enter regularly into our shared daily life. As such, it's an essential core of marital love. Without it, there's no room to grow closer as a couple.

Over the next few years, I had quite a number of little lessons to learn in this area.

The first was that I had to attribute only good motives to Philip's actions. One night, after I had been stewing all day over something he did, I finally nabbed him while he was reading in bed. I accused him of this and that and waited self-righteously for his response. But he just looked me in the eyes and said, "You know, hon, it sure would be nice if you just gave me the benefit of the doubt instead of conjuring up all sorts of hidden motivations for my actions." Then he went back to his book.

I realized what he said was true. I *was* always so eager to go beyond the outward appearances of things and attribute negative motives for everything he did. So I decided not to judge him anymore. There were times when all outward appearances pointed to the contrary, but since I had decided to give him the benefit of the doubt, I never again presumed to know what he was thinking before he told me.

This helped me see the futility of blaming him for things. Solutions to problems never come from establishing whose "fault" it is anyway. Instead, I began to look for ways in which I might be contributing to difficulties between us. And my communication attempts began to be more open to him and more honest about myself. Instead of entering into dialogue with an accusatory attitude, I learned to approach discussions with more of a "Let's see how we can work this out" strategy.

There were other little lessons that followed, such as my decision that I simply would *never* become a nagging wife. But even more, I realized I had no right to try to control my husband, because it wasn't reasonable to dictate to a grown man how he should live his life, what TV shows he could or could not watch, or what he was allowed to think or feel.

This didn't mean I had no right to give input or influence; after all, I've just finished stressing how important communication is. I felt free calmly to make suggestions or to bring things to Philip's attention if I really felt it necessary, because part of love is to seek the other's good. And sometimes this involves building up or loving correction.

But there's a fine line here, sometimes fraught with temptation, between seeking his good and seeking to interfere. Just like God, I had to let my husband exercise his own free will and make his own decisions about his life. I had to let him be! He's a person, after all, and I had to accord to him the same respect for personal freedom as I would want myself.

Even more important to good communication was something else I read from Fulton Sheen: that Christian marriages fail only when spouses fail to be Christian. I realized that I had to treat my husband with the same Christian respect I would extend to any other important person in my life. My behavior and tone of voice and general attitude had to be the same as I would use with a priest or the Pope or Jesus himself.

Understanding the Role of Our Emotions

Now, even with all this in mind, I'd still sometimes get impatient or angry or take things personally. This was discouraging at first, because I didn't understand the proper role of my emotions.

The culture we live in emphasizes emotions and feelings as the basis for living our lives. Instead of using our reason to judge the objective reality of things, to distinguish good from bad, as a tool for making decisions, we ask ourselves how we *feel*. Anything that doesn't feel good must be avoided. If I feel good, things are okay. If I don't feel good, whatever is causing those feelings must be bad.

This affects marital communication in a very significant way: if something feels good to me and not to my spouse, he must be wrong. And if something feels bad to me and not to my spouse, then again, he's wrong! If I put my feelings first, I tend to approach a conversation with a set agenda; since I'm right because I feel this way, he must agree. If he doesn't, I don't need to listen; I need only to convince. Hence, I'm never really *open* to him.

What happens, then, is that underlying realities become obscured. Conflicts can't be resolved. Deadlocks become unbreakable. As we discussed in the chapter about the second P, Person, if I follow my feelings blindly, my intellect isn't doing its job and my will is weakened. I won't be able to discuss a situation reasonably with my husband; instead, I'll remain stuck in an emotional quagmire.

As I became aware of this pitfall, I began to work hard in every conversation, to distinguish among my feelings, my opinions, and what was a fact or a truth. I consciously started sentences with "I feel that," "My opinion on that is," and "The reality of the situation is," in order to train myself and Philip how to discern what the real issues were. This helped us to focus on issues reasonably, without emotional reactions leading the way.

A Harmonious Blending of Viewpoints

Over time, I came to understand another important aspect of communication: that real love manifests itself in a *sincere desire to hear the needs of the other*. I learned to listen attentively in an attempt truly to understand where Philip was coming from, realizing that I couldn't enter into dialogue with him if I simply came with an agenda that I wanted seconded. I couldn't enter into a conversation with the intent to convince and "win" without being open to Philip's legitimate perspective.

But what about when we disagreed? Over time, I realized that it's possible and in fact very common for two well-intentioned people to have differing opinions and outlooks on the same issue. I had to learn to resist my natural assumption of "If I'm right, he must be wrong." It can be that we're both right, but maybe only partially right, and that we are called to synthesize both perspectives to come to a whole and harmonized agreement. I realized that I must never look at Philip as an obstacle to my aims, and that spouses are meant to function in unity, combining their differing perspectives to arrive at the best solution.

A Mother's Rule of Life

The Submission Issue

And here's where the equality-versus-submission issue must be understood. Early on in our marriage, I tended to submit to his decisions because I felt that this was called for in a wife. I'd tell Philip exactly what I thought about it, and then I'd leave the decision up to him. After all, he was the head of the home, and decision-maker was his role as the man of the family, wasn't it?

Philip never agreed with me on this particular idea of "headship." To him, it evoked images of a timid, subservient wife, and a husband who became almost necessarily a semi-tyrant .

He felt that our relationship wasn't healthy if I deferred to his decision-making as a rule, instead of working together with him to reach an agreement. For if it was a rule of thumb, he felt it didn't reflect the reality of our relationship and that it was unnatural. But also, he thought it provided me with an excuse not to become involved, and it presented him with the danger of not really discussing anything; he could just act. There was the temptation to become a petty dictator.

But I had read a lot of books, Catholic and Protestant, about family authority, and I was sure this was what Christian teaching was. So after I told him what I thought, I'd abandon him to let him figure it all out for himself. I must admit that sometimes it seemed such a futile process — telling him what I thought and then watching him turn around and do the opposite. At times, I found it very difficult to "submit" to his decisions — regardless of whether I thought they were made with clear and sound judgment — just because he was the man. But I was submissive to his authority. If it did cause a little anger and resentment to build up within me, I thought I must be wrong to feel that way.

But one day the resentment became so great that I pulled out my *Catechism*. "Okay, let's see where it says I have to submit to his authority!" Well, I couldn't find anything there. The closest thing I could find were sections on authority in general, and these clearly leaned the other way: suggesting that for every authority, there needed to be a "counter-authority" to temper or safeguard against abuse.

I pulled Pope John Paul's *On the Dignity and Vocation of Women* off the shelf, and there I read something that made my mind reel: that there could be no true communion if there wasn't true equality; that it was not a matter of man being superior and woman inferior; that marriage called for mutual submission.

I walked into the kitchen and grabbed the counter edge. John Paul II had just set me free, and I was even angrier than before. It felt as if someone was holding a carrot out in front of my head, the carrot of *power,* and it was all I could do not to reach out and grab that carrot, grab that power that I had given up over and over. For two full days, I battled this desire to assume control, to assert myself and wrest from Philip the control of our marriage. I prayed for strength.

Then my anger left, and I sat Philip down at the kitchen table and read him all the passages that had struck me so profoundly.

It's All About Love, Not Power

Marriage is not about rigid role definitions or about a hierarchy of decision-making responsibilities. It's not about having power *over* each other as spouses. We've seen that the married relationship as God intended is more about becoming one in mind and heart, about the gift of self and being a servant of the other. Authority in marriage is more about leading and helping by example and word, of protecting the one you love, of providing direction and supporting one's spouse and sacrificing self to bring about his or her good. In a word, it's all about love.

And so, yes, Philip and I were both called to mutual submission based on mutual love. The core issue for both of us was whether to *relinquish* or to *retain* our ability to grab at our own desires and preferences over the rights, needs, and interests of the other. I knew that in all things, I was to seek to love him, to give myself to him, to be like Jesus, who emptied himself.

I also realized that I wasn't just to tell Philip my thoughts and leave him to make the decisions. *I was to work them out with him.* For me, this was a call to maturity, to assume mutual responsibility for the direction of our marriage, and not to make Philip a handy scapegoat should things not turn out.

I discovered that our previous way of handling things had prevented full unity. When a woman doesn't feel as if her opinion counts, it's hard to feel as if she counts as a person. Only by acknowledging my full equality, my full human dignity, and my full responsibility within the marriage did I feel a diminishment of resentment in my heart toward Philip and experience a new openness to him.

Dealing with Disagreement

I believe that there are few decisions that need to be made in marriage where a satisfactory compromise can't be reached. If a compromise can't be reached in a serious situation, perhaps it's more an indication that we as a couple aren't ready to make that decision yet, or that there may be other issues in the marriage where we could benefit from outside counsel.

And if we're in complete disagreement? Then Philip and I decide to commit to one or another position, basically deferring to the person who usually deals with the particular issue on a regular basis, or who is better at it. For example, I usually defer to Philip's judgment about vehicle maintenance and repair because he knows about these things. He usually defers to me when it comes to money.

We just had the opportunity to reassess our mortgage. Philip and I both would have loved to have gotten the roof fixed, to have put in cheaper wood heat, to have repaired the windows, and to have done other necessary maintenance. But we didn't want more debt. Now, I'm the one who manages our money because I'm better at it. We have each taken on various responsibilities in our marriage based on our talents and interests, not because of any prearranged method of operation based on gender. After examining all the figures, as well as considering our general goal toward reducing debt, I was reluctant to add on to the mortgage. Philip didn't agree. He thought it would be a sound move to fix the house before it got worse.

But we agreed to do what I thought was best. Why? Because by virtue of the fact that I had taken on this responsibility in our marriage, Philip has developed a level of detachment in this area that allows me to function freely. He deferred to my judgment, after a thorough discussion, of course, because he knows I have a better head for money management.

But we have found that deferring to the other, especially for the person who doesn't fully agree, must be an active decision. The disagreeing spouse can't just go along with it passively, or else resentment can build up. Since it can be difficult to live with the consequences (as I'm sure Philip has and will experience when the oil bill comes), the disagreeing spouse must be prepared consciously and willfully to "own" the decision.

But what if theoretically my husband wasn't that mature? Aside from moral issues or serious safety issues, I would do what I'm still called to do: lovingly submit for the good of the marriage, whether or not I think he's fulfilling his own call to love.

Sex in Marriage

Just as communication is an ongoing channel of grace in our marriage, so, too, are sexual relations between man and wife. Sometimes this reality isn't so clear.

When I first entered marriage, I struggled with sex, somehow believing it was wrong or tainted. I didn't understand why it was that, before marriage, sex was wrong, and then suddenly, after marriage, it was okay. In my heart of hearts, I believed sex itself was sinful.

There were a number of possible reasons I felt this way: perhaps there had been a little bit of prudery passed on to me somewhere; perhaps it was Original Sin rearing its ugly head (for Adam and Eve weren't ashamed of their sexuality until *after* they had sinned); perhaps it was because I had rejected the way sex is flaunted and abused in our society and in the media; perhaps it was because of past personal experiences. Likely it was a combination of some or all of these factors. Whatever the cause, it would take much time and God's direct healing for my attitude to change.

It would also take some serious catechesis and reflection. I read everything I could get my hands on for years, but I found many of my specific questions left unanswered. It was only over time that I came to understand that, contrary to what I had believed before, sex is not a kind of necessary evil, but in fact it is *holy and good*. God created it, for Heaven's sake; not only that, he commanded it: "Be fruitful and multiply"![14] He gave us this gift, good and proper to marriage, to help us express our love to our spouses and to enable us to have children and to propagate the human race.

Based on the Genesis text and what I had synthesized from all my reading, I discovered four basic principles of sexual morality.

[14] Gen. 1:28.

First, sexual activity is meant to be between a man and a woman, according to the intent of God, who created humanity male and female.

Second, it's meant to take place within a lifelong relationship secured by an unbreakable vow, reflecting in our finite way the eternal bond between the Three Persons of the Trinity.

Third, it's meant to be carried out in love, as the Trinity is a relationship of love.

And fourth, it's meant to be open to life in every instance, reflecting God's design that love be fruitful.

To engage in sexual activity outside of these four moral norms is to pervert sex, to alter its intended purpose or use. Our society has misused sex: taken it out of marriage, removed it from love, divorced it from procreation, and enslaved it to pleasure. All sexual sin, out in the world or in our own lives, stems from breaking one or more of these basic norms. All sexual sin is a misuse of a great power God has given us; an insult to the high and wonderful purpose God created sex to have. All sexual sin, then, is in fact *a profanation of something that is holy*.

Sex as a Sacramental Gift

Learning about these moral norms helped me understand better what the Church taught about God's plan for sex, but it didn't completely relieve my discomfort. I knew that I was acting morally, but somehow there was still something missing.

I was having coffee at a friend's house one day when we got to talking about this topic. She shared some of my difficulties in this regard, and we were trying to figure out what the problem was. "I think it boils down to the fact that our society thinks sex is a recreational pastime," she said. She was right, and that got me thinking.

A prevalent modern view of sexuality *is* one of uncommitted, recreational pleasure-seeking. There's an emphasis on the physical, how the body looks and feels. There's a mentality of having sex for what can be derived from it — the sensual experience, the thrills and excitement — all aimed at filling a personal need or desire. Both persons enter into the sexual relationship to get something out of it for themselves. But we know this can't be all there is.

A glance at women's magazines at the supermarket checkout reveals another modern view of sex: as a tool for gaining power. This is a temptation experienced by both men and women: a man experiences it as a desire to dominate; a woman, to manipulate. The granting or withholding of sex becomes a means for getting what one wants from the other — a type of punishment or reward in the relationship. But we know that marital love isn't about power, so sex mustn't be abused in this way.

In reality, the sexual act is one of the actions that effects the grace of the sacrament of Marriage, and that's why there's no complete marriage until it's consummated. Sacraments usually have a physical sign and a hidden reality. To focus only on the outward physical sign of the sex act, to seek sexual pleasure alone, to focus on performance or technique, or even reaching orgasm, is to ignore and threaten the deeper hidden reality of the personal bond, the spiritual communion that's meant to occur.

Sex is, instead, a furthering of my mission to love my spouse. Sexual love has to be, not something I seek solely for myself, but something I *give* — a gift of myself to my husband, an act of tenderness toward his person, and a total reception of him to me. Sex in marriage is really about renewing my wedding vows, my promise to love and cherish him until death. This is important. This gift of self in the sexual act is the normal means by which the grace of the sacrament of Matrimony enters our shared daily lives.

Sexual Integration

The crux of the matter, the unresolved situation that at times weighed heavily upon me, was that I often didn't recognize this "communion of persons" during sex. Sex just seemed physical and not spiritual or personal, and this bothered me. Only later would I see that a truly integrated personal sexual relationship doesn't divorce the physical pleasure as an "accident" of sex, but is a component ordained by God. I realized that the goal was the *blending* of the two — the conscious uniting of the physical and the spiritual — *and that this is a process of integration*, just as in so many other areas of our lives.

Oftentimes, the disintegration experienced between the spiritual and the physical reveals a need for healing within the sexual sphere. Our personal experiences of sexual immorality, or sexual abuse, or coercion of any kind done to us, all interfere with our ability to give ourselves freely to our husbands and to experience sex as love.

Sometimes we may not understand what the issue is, but there's just "something wrong," something blocking full sexual, emotional, and spiritual communion with our husbands. Again, it's always good to seek counseling in order to talk out any damage that has been done to us or by us. I've also experienced direct healing from God in this area, as a result of healing prayers by a priest. There has been no stronger indication to me of the holiness and approval of God for marital sexual relations than his divine intervention to promote full sexual unity between my husband and me.

But in the meantime, I realized any dark nights of "not seeing" the spiritual reality of conjugal love calls for an act of faith, just like any other sacrament. The physical union of man and woman in marriage is a foreshadowing of the spiritual communion God brings about between us. Occasionally I get an inkling of this, a moment of truth and vision, but many times, as with the other sac-raments, I can't consciously see the deeper reality of our spiritual love during lovemaking.

～

As regards my Rule, practically speaking I didn't feel there was much in the way of concrete duties involving Philip. So, to make him a conscious priority in my life, I had to look a little deeper. I remembered something Pope John Paul had said many years ago, that love could be defined as "availability, acceptance, and help." So, this was where I started.

How could I be more available to my husband? This was a time issue. Since Philip worked outside the home all day, five days a week, the actual time I had to spend with him was limited. I began by clearing my evenings of excess commitments so I could be physically present when he was home from work. After the kids were in bed, I decided, I'd have no set plans for most evenings of the week, so that I could be available to him.

Now, many nights Philip spent doing his school prep, but this didn't matter. The important thing was for me to be ready to be with him without having any other pressing needs. I might have projects I wanted to work on, or a good show I wanted to watch, but in my Rule, if Philip needed to talk or simply wanted to spend time with me, that held top priority.

I also basically reserved Saturday nights for him. That was the night we would have our dates! Given our often limited finances, this didn't mean an expensive night out on the town. I asked a couple of friends how they made time for their husbands, and I heard wonderful little ideas for making a special time at home — from barbequing steaks and having a glass of wine, to popcorn and a video, to playing cards or even reading together. So I'd keep this in mind when I did my grocery shopping. If he wanted to go out with a friend, that was fine, too. There were always lots of little things I could do to fill up an at-home-alone Saturday night! The key was simply to be available and to allow for free time to be spontaneous with him.

Next in my Rule, I focused on John Paul II's notion of acceptance. I decided that I would consciously focus on an attitude of basic kindness and courtesy with every word that came from my mouth. I also decided to be purposefully more encouraging and to give him my whole attention every time we seriously talked. I also began to teach the children not to interrupt us if we were talking.

And the final criterion, help, was simple. There was very little practical help I could offer outside my normal motherly and domestic tasks. But I did find some little things to include: making sure there was a pot of coffee on in the morning and filling up Philip's coffee cup for the drive to work, setting out his lunch, and telling him his options for breakfast (he usually made his own).

Working Out Your Essentials

Here you'll want to focus on the practical help your husband needs from you on a daily basis and on the time you make available to spend with him. Keep it simple. Ask yourself:

• *When can I open up a regular chunk of time just to be available to my husband? What types of things can I arrange, such as regular time out together, or special nights "in," which will break up the humdrum of daily routines and help us both to relax?* Write these down.

• *Does my husband need any help from me aside from housework? Are there any little things he appreciates, ways I could help him make his life a little easier? Does he need any assistance from me in his work?*

A Mother's Rule of Life

When can I schedule these things in? What days? What time of day?
Write these down.

Beyond the Basics

Regardless of what you've scheduled, the heart of the Rule regarding your husband is the relationship you have with him. Taking time to think and assess your marriage is important; in fact, it doesn't hurt to set aside time on a regular basis to do this, both by yourself and with your husband if possible (although I realize that not all husbands enjoy long discussions about marriage!).

When you begin, try to focus on what *you* can change or do, not so much on what *your husband* necessarily needs to change. Sometimes our husbands' faults seem very obvious to us, and yet we don't really see our own. But remember, we can't "command" a change in our husbands, just as we can't instantly change our own hearts. The best way to effect any real healthy difference in our marriages is to work on our own faults and behaviors first. As I mentioned earlier, Pope Paul VI said that the greatest form of evangelization is the witness of our own example, and only secondly, our words. If we remove the log from our own eyes first, maybe we will have a clearer indication of how to help our husband with his splinter.

Think about the main areas mentioned in this chapter, and consider whether there any obstacles to good communication in your marriage? Is there anything you're doing that makes your husband reluctant to talk? Think about how you can change that. Is there anything you need to do positively, such as to be more attentive or more positive when you speak with your husband?

Are there any areas where you need to forgive your husband? Any areas in your marriage where you and your husband need to clear the air or resolve differences?

Think about how you can serve your husband better. Are there any little things you can do to show him you love him? In what ways do you pray for your husband? Does he need more prayer?

Are there any areas in your sex life that need to be aligned more fully with the moral norms of sexuality in marriage? Are there any attitude shifts you need to make in order for sex to be truly as a gift of yourself to your husband? Is there a need for healing or repentance in this area? Is there need of any counsel from an objective outside source?

Are you taking full responsibility with your husband in all spheres of your marriage? Is there any area you're shirking? Is there any part of your marriage in which you're being controlling? How can you change?

Ask the Holy Spirit to show you what he intends for you and your husband and to reveal to you any areas that are in need of improvement.

⁓

The third priority in marriage, Partner, calls us to a mission toward our husband. We need to focus on loving and helping him by our attention, by our support, and by sharing our unique person with him. It isn't that we can't desire our husband's love, nor rely on him in our weakness, nor seek his encouragement or consolation with our legitimate personal needs. All of these are necessary and as God intends. But the third P also clearly encourages us to adopt our special *assignment* as a wife — actively to decide to love and to become a conscious channel of grace for our spouse.

Mother Teresa often counseled her nuns to seek to love more than to be loved, to understand more than to be understood, to serve more than to be served. And in her work with the poor, she said, she often received far more than she gave.

Chapter 6

⁀

The Fourth P: Parent

In the fourth P, Parent, we're called to attend to the duties inherent in being a parent. Just as we're called to love our husbands actively, so, too, we're to adopt as a mission the *second purpose* of the sacrament of Marriage: begetting and raising children. By virtue of the special consecration we discussed in the third P, God has empowered us actively to love our children and to fulfill our duty as their primary educators.

A Hidden Disrespect for My Mothering Vocation

While on my maternity leave, one day I was out walking my daughter in her stroller. I was heading down the street to visit my husband, who was teaching at a local high school. I reached the school as the final bell rang, and out poured tons of teenagers.

At that moment, I became very self-conscious and felt my face flush. I experienced a very deep and strange emotion: I was embarrassed. Embarrassed! And all because I was seen pushing a baby stroller! It seemed very clear to me at the time that this was something to be ashamed of. All my education and training counted for nothing in my eyes because even an uneducated teenager could push a baby stroller. It seemed to me I was a failure because I wasn't out working at something "important."

I was a bit surprised to realize that I really didn't think much of this mothering vocation in the first place. I discovered that I really felt as if I was only a housekeeper and a babysitter, and I believed I could be replaced — that anyone could come in and raise my children just as well as I could.

A Difficult and Unexpected Choice

One day, when my six-month maternity leave was almost up, my principal called and re-offered to me the teaching position I had held the previous year.

"I don't know . . ." I replied. Gee, I hadn't even thought about going back to work yet, and Philip and I hadn't discussed it.

"Well, I really can't wait on this, Holly," he replied. "I need to know now."

Conflict raged inside me. We were still new to Calgary, and it was still strange to us. I had no family available for childcare, nor any friends who stayed at home. I wanted to work, but I wasn't sure whether I could leave my baby. I needed time to think.

"I need to talk it over with my husband," I replied.

"I'm sorry, Holly. I don't have time to wait. Do you want the job or not? I need a yes or no," the principal countered.

Remembering something Philip had once told me about the wisdom of never being pushed into making a decision, especially if it couldn't first be discussed with your spouse, I gave him my answer: "Okay, then, I guess the answer is no."

Hanging up the phone, I realized I had just had my whole life turned around in a flash without warning. I was suddenly headed in a completely different direction from the one I had been traveling in for years.

Why had God led me in the direction of teaching, I wondered, if I wasn't going to be a teacher?

At that moment, I had to make one major act of hope that God knew what he was doing, and I'm not sure I succeeded in it! But I came across something the missionary Elizabeth Elliot had said that tided me over until I could understand better. She said we need to learn to be able to sacrifice even good things for a higher purpose; that although we all understand why weeds need to be pulled from a garden, it isn't so easy to understand why flowers themselves die. She said that in God's wisdom, even the petals on a flower must die, even though they're beautiful. And with this, I understood that *even what is good must be sacrificed sometimes, for the sake of a greater good.*

I understood there was a priority of goods and that the calling of my vocation took precedence over my career pursuits. My family needs were to come first in my life. I knew this basic principle had to guide how I spent my time and effort. At that point and in those circumstances, my little baby needed me at home. For all of us, in our Rule, we need to accord to our children the necessary time and attention required to meet their needs.

A Culture Shock

I experienced a tremendous culture shock. All my training and experience had geared me to assume a position in the workplace. So when I stayed home, I felt as if life was meaningless and that I had no real purpose. I remember watching little children from the neighborhood walk by my window in the morning on their way to school, lunchboxes in hand and school bags over shoulders, laughing and chatting away, and I would be overcome with sadness. I was jealous of children! I wanted to go to school, too, and I felt somehow penalized and imprisoned in my isolated little world at home. Everything I was, everything I had developed myself for, and everything I wanted to do just flew out the window. At one point, I said to Philip, "I feel as if I've given up everything except my life, my faith, and my family." I felt as if a great big part of me had died.

I mourned my teaching career, something I had felt called to by God, and yet I saw a deeper need of the heart and a new call from God to be at home with my child. This led to a split of mind and heart that took many years of reading and researching, praying and pondering, sacraments and God's direct healing to help me overcome.

It took a long time for me to realize I had been *chosen by God* to be a mother and that I myself had chosen to be a mother. It took a while to see that, yes, my talents and interests and training were all important things, but would override any calling outside my family for a good long while.

And I'd come to learn, slowly, that the seemingly mundane and unimportant work of a mother — loving God, living a holy marriage, and raising happy, balanced, holy children — was in the grand scheme of God's plan more important than the many projects and ambitions I had in other areas. I had to learn, over the course of years, that relationships were more important than tasks, that *being* was more important than *doing*.

Discovering the Mission of Motherhood

For in reality, we're called to the mission of motherhood. But it was something I hadn't previously thought of.

I stayed home with our growing family for the next few years, but often found myself bored and restless. I didn't exactly know what I was supposed to *do* with the children. I still felt as if I were only "watching" them. I felt as if I was in a job for which I had never been trained. I certainly saw no mission inherent in motherhood. I couldn't even look back over my childhood for a reference point in my case, because, between my being ill as a youngster and sleeping a lot, and my mother working full time, I had no model of an at-home mom I could imitate or relate to.

Then along came an opportunity. By the providence of God, I was offered a part-time position as a catechetics director at a large parish in a nearby city. I grabbed it, not only because I really wanted it, but so that I could hop into what I considered at the time a more normal lifestyle, one that I would be familiar with.

That first year was sheer bliss. It was so good to get out and do something "meaningful," instead of just housework and reading stories to little ones. The only thing I found difficult was leaving my little ones with their caretaker, especially two-year-old Nicki, who would sit, elbows on knees, head bowed down, as I drove away. My heart went out to him, but I squelched the feelings of guilt and pain and left him anyway. Then, on my days off, he would be very aggressive with me. It would take me the rest of the week to get him back to being himself, only to start the cycle again.

However, I found the catechetics work challenging and inspiring, and I flung myself headlong into it. As time went on, I was beginning to notice the tremendous needs of the children I was working with. It was frustrating, having to dictate basic prayers to eighth-grade students who had never heard them before. I remember a sixth-grade class that didn't even know about King Herod, much less that he was after the Baby Jesus, or that Mary and Joseph had to flee to Egypt to escape him. I was stupefied that after years of catechism classes, children didn't know who the Pope was, defined *grace* as the prayer said before supper, and couldn't identify the three Persons of the Blessed Trinity.

The needs were so great, and I began to suspect my efforts were a superficial solution, a mere Band-Aid trying to cover a deep wound in today's families. I saw plainly that many parents were not leading their own children in the Faith and were thinking that the catechetics program, for one hour a week, twenty weeks a year, was doing the job. Let me tell you, it wasn't! I began to wonder whether what I was doing was *really* meaningful. I wasn't able to address the deeper problems; I couldn't spend more time with these kids. Parents had to be the primary educators of their children; I couldn't replace them. Finally, in exasperation I asked myself, "What *can* I do that will really make a difference in society?"

And the answer led me right back to my own home.

Raising my own children with a Christian worldview was the biggest contribution to society that I could possibly make; giving to the world healthy, holy citizens who would spread their influence in an exponential way that I couldn't accomplish with my paltry efforts alone. My work with my children was the very core of societal change. I had discovered the *mission* of motherhood!

I knew I couldn't focus on this mission and still do the type of work I was doing at the parish. The catechetics work was intensive and involved great responsibilities and much mental concentration. I had already experienced great stress in trying to fulfill just the essentials of both jobs. It was with great sadness that I turned in my resignation, but I knew I had a more important job to do with my own children at home.

The Beauty and Dignity of Parenthood

As soon as I stopped working outside the home, Nicholas calmed down and became happier. He had just needed *me*. I was not replaceable! I myself was personally called to be with my children; God had given my children to *me*, not to anyone else. In God's design, my uniqueness was tailor-made for my unique children. So I was inspired to study motherhood more intently, wanting to find out all I could about it. Soon I came across a teaching that completely changed my outlook.

Philip and I were scheduled to speak to a marriage-prep group one winter, and in the marriage manual, we came across the claim that "parents image God's work at creation." Hmm . . . that was an interesting thought! I dug out my Bible and turned to Genesis and wondered, "Just what did God *do* at creation, anyway?" As I read, it was as if a veil were lifted; I could see clearly God's intent for parenting from the beginning. I had always known that Philip and I were participating in the work of God by being open to life and having children. But I hadn't realized that *everything I do as a parent* was in fact imaging God's work.

It was clear enough that just as God provided food and shelter and everything Adam and Eve needed to live and survive, so, too, Philip and I were called to provide food and shelter. But I also noted that God created a *paradise*, and so my home was called to be a mini-paradise, a place of beauty and peace and harmony.

Just as God walked and talked with Adam and Eve, so, too, I was called to be in loving relationship and close communication with my children.

As God infused knowledge into Adam and Eve for survival and for stewardship of creation, so, too, I was called to educate my children, to share with them the gift of faith I had received, to teach them the skills and understanding they needed to live in society and make it a better place.

I realized that just as God gave Adam and Eve the task of caring for the garden, so, too, I was to train my children to work and delegate responsibility to them in order to build character and to give them a role in the care of our home.

As God governed Adam and Eve, giving them a Rule and enforcing it, so, too, Philip and I were called to govern our children, leading and disciplining them. And just as God forgave the race of Adam and Eve for their rebellion, and as he bent down and fashioned clothing for them, so, too, I was to forgive my children any trespasses and cover their sins with love. But, since Adam and Eve still had to leave the garden for their own good, I recognized that I mustn't unnecessarily shield my children from the just consequences of their actions.

We can see from this that *parents image the work of God at creation*. What a lofty and exciting vocation we have! What dignity was attached to even the most apparently mundane task! Every action we do for or with our children reflects the divine love God showed at creation. My own ignorance of my vocation had hampered me from seeing its beauty before. But now the truth had set me free. No longer did I feel as if I was doing something of lesser importance.

We have a real, important, irreplaceable mission — a *personal mission* to raise our children. As Pope John Paul II says in his *Letter to Families*, "raising children can be considered a genuine apostolate."[15]

Providing a Catholic Education

This mission meant that I was called to raise my children *actively*, not merely to "watch" them like a nanny. Who else was going to teach them all they needed to know in this life? Who was going to lead them to God if Philip and I didn't do it? Together with my husband, *I* was the formative influence in my children's lives. *I* was the one who was called to mold and form them and prepare them for this world and the next. *I* was the primary educator of my children. This was a privilege I would never again undervalue.

[15] No. 16.

The next question was *how* was I to raise them? I knew I was to provide a Catholic education for the children, but there were no Catholic schools in our area. So, because of this circumstance, because I knew I had the desire and skills necessary to do it, and because I believed God was asking it of our family, we began to homeschool. I eagerly researched the branches of knowledge and educational thought and began to pull together what I decided was a balanced and complete curriculum, which I continued to fine-tune over the years.

As mothers, as parents, we need to realize that in any education, academic excellence, a broad necessary knowledge base, and thorough intellectual training are essential. To ensure the provision of these things, either through homeschooling or the choice of a good school, is a responsibility of our vocation.

But as those early months passed, I began to sense that there must be more to it. What did it mean for Philip and me — as *parents,* not as teachers — to be the primary educators of our children? What did it mean to provide for them a truly Catholic education? It had to be about more than just math or reading lessons, more than academics alone. I began what would become a years-long search for the answers.

Over time, the answer came: parenting is a call to form *persons.* We're called to bring God to our children's spirits, truth to their minds, health to their bodies, skill to their hands, beauty and creativity to their hearts, and in all this, virtue to their wills and sanctity to their souls. The education we are to provide has to go beyond the three *R*s and beyond professional or vocational training.

"Education consists essentially in preparing man for what he must *be*, and for what he must *do* here below, in order to attain the sublime end for which he was created," wrote Pope Pius XI. This education, then, has both *natural* and *supernatural* goals. Recognition of the supernatural goals — expressed in an emphasis on religious and moral formation — is what makes a truly Catholic education distinct.

Known by many names — catechesis, character development, will training, practicing virtue, self-discipline — moral and religious training invites our children to *follow Jesus and always to choose good and avoid evil.* This is the heart of moral perfection and the heart of the Christian educative process. This isn't confined to any classroom, but permeates the child's entire life. It's a training of the will and reason over the emotions, which we discussed in the "Person" chapter.

All this means that the goal of a true education is to inspire our children to become saints! And so religious education and ethics and virtue and morality have to become the core of our teaching as parents. Our children's experience of the entire world of knowledge is to be framed within the Christian worldview, through grace.

I found all of this an inspiring goal, but how was I to implement it? I had to get practical.

Putting Children in Touch with God

I've found that I can talk to my kids about God until I'm blue in the face, but by itself, it often makes no difference. Like us, kids need to have direct contact with God. Our first job is always to help provide our children with access to God's grace. We can do this in many ways: by getting them to Mass and Confession regularly, by making individual and family prayer a normal part of their daily life, and by getting them a Bible and other prayer aids to encourage them. And, of course, we can pray for them always.

In addition, we can teach them the Faith, answering questions about what we believe and why. We can share inspiring tales of saints and virtue, through books and magazines and Catholic comic books and saint videos — anything that will attract their interest and have them reading and watching. We can also strive to immerse them in a loving Christian culture by establishing a harmonious home and meaningful Christian family traditions: feast-day celebrations, Baptism day parties, special foods and crafts, and other practices organized around the key liturgical cycles of the year.

All these practices are a good start, but there's still more to be done.

Becoming an Example, a Living Witness

One day I heard eight-year-old Anna speaking rather impatiently to a younger sibling, and I noted uncomfortably that she sounded just like me! Our children imitate us, even down to the way we speak, so how much more will they look to us as models for how to live! Our children need to see us living our faith fully, to see our worldview permeated by Christian truth, and to see our fidelity to the moral norms of the Faith. This extends to everything from belief in the Eucharist right down to making our bed when we get up. It even extends to our attitudes, for we can hardly teach a willing spirit and uncomplaining cheerfulness if we groan every time we have to wipe up a spill or kneel down to pray!

Thus, living out my vocation as parent means careful attention to the first three Ps. We can't pass down a faith or a moral code or a serene spirit if we don't practice it ourselves. And we can't model virtue in relationships if we don't exhibit it in our marriage. This calls for a constant recommitment to our own ongoing conversion, our own self-control, our own prayer and reliance on God. If I can't follow my own Rule, I can't expect much of the children.

Being a Channel of God's Love

Our love for our children must reflect God's relationship with Adam and Eve. In the words of Pope John Paul II, we need to be more available and accepting of them in heart and mind and body. And we have to love them by doing what's best for them.

Being *available* meant I had to tone down all the thoughts and projects that constantly filled my head and make time and room for my children in my busy life. I had to be able to stop what I was doing, take the time to look each of them in the eye, listen to them, and respond. I couldn't just rush through my contact with them on the way to something more "important." No more absentminded "Yes, yes, dear, whatever you want . . ." only to proceed on to my next interest, oblivious to their presence or their needs.

I also needed to be more *accepting* of them. Each one was designed by God as a unique person. I needed to spend time with them and truly get to know each of my children, to discover their unique talents and interests, their individual strengths and weaknesses. Only then could I encourage them in the ways they needed and help them overcome their troubles.

And in loving them, I had to do what was *best* for them. This simplified everything for me. Was too much junk food best for them? Was being allowed to hit each other best for them? Was staying up late too often or sleeping in every day or never doing chores best for them? And even when they'd worked hard for weeks and were becoming apathetic, worn out, and discouraged by the never-ending monotony of math and English, could I still consider a strict adherence to the schedule as *best* for them? Wouldn't a day off, some spontaneous and creative activity, be best to help lift up their spirits and refresh them?

I knew I'd sometimes encounter resistance; children obviously don't *always* want what's best for them! I believed if I based my decisions for my children on a higher law and more virtuous priorities, instead of on their childish whims or my selfish desires, they'd understand (even if it took a little explaining) that I was only seeking their *good*, and they would eventually love this. If they knew I was *really* only acting in their best interests, they'd be almost compelled to follow me because children are more than willing to follow an inspiring leader. Thus, the challenge was on me: to win the trust and loyalty of my children by truly striving always to do what was best for them.

Perhaps the simplest of all, yet often the most difficult, I could show my love and mirror God's love for them by how I treated them. Too often I had found myself speaking more respectfully to strangers and adults than to my own children. But loving our children means treating them with the same amount of courtesy, respect, and politeness with which we want to be treated, or as we would treat any adult, or the Pope or Mother Teresa, or the Lord himself.

Where I have failed in this, I have taken it to Confession.

Authority to Discipline Our Children

For a long time, I had been unsure about what the truly Christian notion of authority was. Too often I knew it was confused with "authoritarianism," and I didn't want to exert power and control over my children in this manner. I didn't want fear of me or fear of punishment to be the sole motive for good behavior, as it had often been for me when I was a child. I was still a youth when I knew that fear and punishment had not taught me any moral lessons, nor had it led me to assume responsibility for my own actions. Instead, it only gave me an excuse to hide and sneak around and lie and try not to get caught. And eventually, it led to rebellion.

No, I wanted more for my children and for me as a parent. I'd ponder how the Blessed Mother raised Jesus; surely it wasn't through yelling and hollering, through threat or punishment. Perhaps it was more like Miss Duffy, my second-grade teacher. Miss Duffy was just plain sweet. She did nothing but smile and make me feel good. One day I lied to her and told her I had finished my math work so I could help her paste the stars on our "reward moons" on the cloakroom door. When she found out about my fib, she brought me to her desk, pulled out her wooden spoon, and dutifully tapped my hand. I smiled. Even her punishment was soft and merciful. Did she really think that hurt?

But then I looked into her eyes. No, it wouldn't be the severity of the punishment that taught me to finish my math and never to lie to Miss Duffy again. It was that I never wanted to see that look of hurt and disappointment on her face again.

As parents, we've been invested with authority by God to lead and make disciples of our children. The word *disciple* is derived from *discipulus*, meaning "student." Hence, the basis of all discipline is to teach, or more appropriately in relation to the parent role, to apprentice my children in life. This, too, begins by witnessing virtue to my children and living out a loving relationship with them.

But apprenticing them is an even more conscious and active process. As a plumber takes on an assistant, shows him the jobs to be done, explains how to do it, and slowly gives the apprentice more and more hands-on responsibility, so are parents called to lead their children. I had to live life *with* my children, having them participate in much that I do, guiding and explaining, letting them try things, and slowly issuing more and more responsibility to them to assume for themselves.

This can be very practical. As I clean the kitchen, I get them to clean with me, explaining how to do it, letting them try, and eventually, when they've achieved competence, assigning them tasks to assume on their own. So, too, in our prayer lives. I invite them to pray with me, discuss it, show them, explain, and slowly encourage them to try it on their own as well as during prayer time with the family.

The authority of parents also includes the ability to make decisions for the family and to expect these to be upheld and obeyed. These decisions are not to be made on the basis of our selfish whims or arbitrary desires, or out of a mere habit of giving commands. Our authority given by God resides in the right and duty to make decisions based on the higher moral laws that both parents and children are subject to obey. As such, what we ask our children to do must be based on a real, legitimate reason, *on a real good for the benefit of the child, the parent, and the common good of the family.*

This is why we have the right to say, "No hitting," "No stealing," and "No talking back"; because all of us are under command from God to love each other. Explaining the justifiable reasons for our requests and even our commands is not only practically necessary for a parent to do; it is our children's *right* to know why we ask it. The explanations we give become occasions for our children to learn and grow.

Fostering Obedience

What's expected of our children must be well explained, totally clear to them, and properly supervised, with parental assistance if needed. We must be involved with our children's attempts to do what they ought, helping them in any way that they can't fulfill on their own.

But if a child refuses to comply with our legitimate commands, we as parents have the duty to ensure we're obeyed. There's no service of love done to a child who's permitted to have his own way all the time. Disobedience and selfishness reflect the sin of Adam more than the virtue of Christ. And if I as a parent don't teach my children to obey, who will? How will they ever be disciplined enough to fulfill the duties required by their employers? If they won't obey their mother, whom they see, how will they learn to obey their God, whom they don't see?

There are a number of consequences that can occur if a child refuses to comply. We can have a little chat and explain what God expects of his children and why, for it's the religious motive that's often the most meaningful and most efficacious. We can also warn the child about what he's doing, just as God did with Cain, and encourage him to change his mind (remembering to tell him we're proud of him when he does). We can send him to another room until he's ready to come back and obey, for as Dostoevsky noted in *Crime and Punishment*, the worst consequence of all it to be "placed outside the company of men." We can suspend privileges for a time, or we can just let natural consequences take their course — he probably won't touch that hot stove again. And sometimes, we just need to stand firm, insist, and wait them out. When a child realizes that this situation just isn't going to go away, oftentimes he'll change his mind.

What's very important, though, is that the child must make the decision to obey. Free will is a gift from God and not something we have a right to take away. It's better that we permit the child to accept the negative consequence of disobedience than to abuse his will by forcing him to comply. It can be as simple as "Okay, if you won't clean your bedroom this morning as I've asked, that's your decision, but don't expect any computer time or TV or phone time until it's done." Or we can give him more *time to decide:* "Why don't you go out to the porch and come back in when you're ready to clean up your painting supplies."

So we want to encourage obedience and insist if necessary, but always permit the child to opt for a logical consequence. We must respect his freedom. That's what God does.

It's also important to distinguish here between isolated acts of disobedience and a general habit of rebellious behavior. With the latter, there are often deeper, underlying factors that need to be examined before rushing into any punitive response. There's always a reason for a pattern of misbehavior. It could be something I, as a parent, am doing: being overbearing or too demanding or not listening well. The child could have his own personal problems, such as teenage mood swings, frustrations with friends, or loneliness. Rebelliousness as a habit can be a sign of discouragement and seeking attention in whatever way it can be gotten, be it good or bad. There can even be physical reasons: lack of sleep, improper nutrition, or an underlying medical condition.

The important thing here is to discover and work on the root causes of negative external behavior. Make sure the child practices good habits when it comes to getting enough sleep, proper nutrition, ample recreation, and a satisfying work routine to develop energy and vigor. Have good conversations, talk with the child about his problems, and foster an encouraging, loving relationship. A little attention and love, understanding and compassion can radically change a child's general attitude. Let him know he's "good" and Mummy sees him as good. So often children rise to meet the level of our expectations. If we secretly think of them as rebels, they tend to act like rebels.

Mummy Must Mean What She Says and Enforce It
To influence our children and train them properly, the lesson I have most needed to learn is to be consistent. This can be difficult! Sometimes it would have been much easier to let them

ignore me or run off when I told them to do something. It can be a real pain to have to get up off the couch or put my coffee down to go ensure that what I said was being done. And sometimes I'd feel as if I had battle fatigue! I know I've had what seemed like whole seasons of working very hard to keep the children in line, and often felt as if I were failing.

But I realized that, if I didn't supervise and ensure obedience to me, I was in great part to blame for my children's ignoring me from time to time. It all boiled down to a little motto: "Mummy means what she says and is willing to enforce it." My children need to *know* that Mummy's words aren't hollow and meaningless.

But most important, I have had to repeat this motto over and over for *my* benefit. "Mummy means what she says. . . ." First, I had to make sure that what I was asking them to do was reasonable and justified. This helped me cut back on any unnecessary demands I placed on my children and reduced the number of incidents that could be interpreted as a challenge by a child.

". . . And is willing to enforce it." So second, I had to *take the time* to deal with those things that were legitimate commands, those things that they *ought* to do. Too many times we're distracted and busy, and so we only half-heartedly deal with noncompliant behavior. But this only teaches our children to ignore us when we're ignoring them and causes the behavior to escalate. Instead, I find I'm most successful when I drop everything else, look them in the eye, and give them my full attention. Stress is diminished, because disobedience doesn't grow to a point where it becomes unmanageable.

Now, I've heard people groan and complain about their own inconsistency, and this is something I understand intimately! But really, consistency is merely a habit, and a habit is formed by exercising the will; it calls for a decision, repeated over and over again, and begins one step at a time. We discussed this in the second P, Person. And as with any habit, consistency does become easier. We need to foster the firm conviction that training our children is absolutely essential — a responsibility of our vocation. If I can't be bothered to make my children obey, why would they bother either?

So we must make the effort to do what we ought, so that our children will do what they ought. And it *is* an effort. I've often wondered if this isn't what Scripture is talking about when it says mothers are saved through their children! As we work to form and mold our children, they, in turn, force us to face, and, we hope, to master, our own weaknesses. In parenting, saving grace is a two-way street.

Christian Freedom for Children

And finally, I realized the goal of all moral training was to prepare my children to assume complete responsibility for themselves. We discussed this in the second P, Person, that freedom is "taking on responsibility for who you are to become." God calls everyone to freedom, children too, according to their growing capacities to use it.

In addition, I didn't want my children to be dependent on Mummy to tell them what they could or could not do, but gradually to develop an inner moral compass that would point them in the right direction — not out of fear, but out of love. The desire for goodness must come from their own hearts. My role was to nurture that desire.

This is called "freedom within limits." We give our children an arena in which to learn how to make good decisions. We can offer them options in which they're free to choose, such as *when* they can make time for prayer given their daily needs, instead of scheduling it for them, or what *type* of prayer they feel drawn to, instead of parental insistence upon a certain devotion. What's important to parents is *that* their children pray — how or when can be left up to the child. In any situation where they can exercise their reason and choose a real moral good that truly suits their personality and circumstances, we're encouraging the process of personal order.

Perhaps I might have to help them discern their options, to define what's good and what's not, to show what the consequences of any action might be in any given circumstances; but in the end, I have to give them the same freedom God gave them to exercise their own free will, to choose; to choose the good — and to choose God.

⌒

Any teacher knows that the development of routines is essential to maintaining classroom discipline. Routines have been called "preventative discipline," since they serve to curb bad behavior before it has a chance to happen. Routines enable children to know what to do, when to do it, where to do it, and how to do it. Children then form orderly habits, which lend themselves to orderly conduct, which sets the stage for learning. Elementary classroom teachers actually teach these routines and supervise their fulfillment early on in the year until the children are doing them properly. Then, when competence is reached, the teacher is free to move into more academic pursuits. For there can be no true learning when the children's behavior and environment are chaotic.

I realized I could take these skills I had learned as a teacher and apply them at home. So I began to figure out where I could develop routines that met the personal needs of my children.

I started with little things. What were the hygiene tasks my children needed to accomplish each day? I made a detailed list.

Then I made sure they had appropriate access to the supplies they needed, such as toothbrushes and shampoo and laundry hampers, so that they knew where to find and where to put things. I took my children around and explained, "From now on, your toothbrushes go here, and we put the cap back on the toothpaste, and your laundry can go in the hamper at the top of the stairs, and . . ." I proceeded to go through all the hygiene, laundry, and clothing tasks, then eventually prayer and study duties, in this fashion.

Thus, I had to find a logical place for everything, and I had to teach this to my children. Rosaries were hung on the rosary cross in the living room. Bibles were beside their beds. School books went in that bookshelf only. Clean laundry went in these drawers. Coats and hats went here. Boots went there.

A little boy who was visiting one day got a splinter in his finger. I said, "Go get me the needle stuck in the post by the mirror between the two kitchen windows."

He got it and came back saying, "What's this needle for?"

"Why, splinters, of course!" I said.

He replied in awe, "Boy! You sure do have a place for everything around here, don't you!"

After I had figured out a place for everything and had gotten the children (and my husband) on board, I had to figure out a *time* for everything. Initially I would say, "At 7:30, you can get up and do this . . ." But really, the heart of routine is natural *progression:* X simply leads to Y, and Z follows it. Morning tidying comes before breakfast, which is followed by kitchen cleanup. It has to be logical and as close to the natural rhythm as possible. Well, hygiene before or after meals and just before bedtime sounded right. Folding the clean laundry and putting the dirty in the hamper could be dealt with just before bedtime when the kids got changed. School would take place most of the morning, and then after lunch for a while. Group prayer was after breakfast, and before bedtime, and formal catechesis would take place on certain days.

And then in my Mother's Rule, I had to set aside time to supervise these tasks and ensure that they were completed. I also wrote out tasks and routines on charts, laminated them so they wouldn't get gooey and force me continually to redo them, and posted them in the appropriate places around the house. For example, in the bathroom there were charts that said "Brush teeth. Wash face and hands. Comb hair. Put toothpaste away. Wipe counter." For the little ones who couldn't read, I drew pictures.

It's important to realize that, children being children, this teaching and supervising process doesn't ever totally end. Sometimes we get a little break, but eventually we have to go back and reteach them. This is really just part of Mummy's ongoing job! It's also not a sign of failure that we need to keep teaching and supervising our children. Teachers in the classroom do this all year, every year, too. All training takes time.

Working Out Your Essentials

Here you want to figure out what your children need to do on a regular basis and ensure it's accomplished. We'll deal with chores in more detail in the next chapter, but here you can include their personal chores and private rooms. For their persons, the same categories we used for ourselves and our needs in the "Person" chapter apply. Remember, you're dealing with *essential tasks* here; try to keep it as simple as possible.

• *What exactly do your children need to do? For daily hygiene? To deal with their clothing? Their personal prayer? Sports and hobbies? Friends? Catechism and Mass and Confession? Homework or schooling? Sleep and rest? Exercise?* Make lists, and write these down.

+ *What supplies or materials do your children need to do these things?*

+ *Where do their things belong?* Put everything in a logical place, and teach it to your children (and your husband!).

+ *When can your children perform these duties or activities? With older children, have them sit down with you and go over it with them. For little ones, decide on your own.* Figure out the logical time for these activities to occur in your home and family, and write them down.

Make up any charts you need, and post them. Coat, boot, and hat procedures can go in the porch. Laundry procedures can go in the bedroom by the dressers. Show them to your children. This will free your children from having to remember all the duties they need to do. You can always say, "What does your chart say?" or you can read it out loud for your little ones.

Over time, you'll notice that there are other little tasks that you didn't include. You can either decide to let these things come up randomly, or you can write them down and alter your schedule or posters if need be. The more you account for, the less stress you and your children will experience.

+ *When can I help my children?* You'll need to set aside time every day to help your children fulfill what they need to do, depending on their age and level of maturity. Give yourself and the children ample time so that you won't feel rushed. You can always reduce the scheduled time later, once you all get the hang of it and develop new habits.

Beyond the Basics

Here, we really reach the core of our responsibilities to our children, those things that can't be scheduled. Perhaps the best way to start is to watch the children as they learn to follow the routines you've set up in your home. *How* are they doing their work? Are they confused and unsure? Are they complaining? Doing it grudgingly? Sneaking away when you're not looking? Doing a sloppy job?

Once you've examined how they're working, you want to figure out *why* they're behaving that way. Through conversation, prayer, and thought, discern what the real issue is. If they're confused, perhaps they need more teaching and modeling. If they're complaining, perhaps your expectations need to be revised. Perhaps you need to help motivate them by giving them something to look forward to. If they're doing it grudgingly, maybe you need to teach them about the importance of what they're doing, how they're fulfilling God's will by taking care of themselves. Maybe they could be encouraged to offer it up and to hear you commiserate with their suffering. Maybe you need to give them some input as to how they could make things better and discuss the options.

Are they sneaking away when you're not looking? Maybe they need to make a freedom-within-limits choice. Is there a time they consider better to fulfill this task?

Are they doing a sloppy job? Perhaps you could seek to inspire them to do their best; read them stories about people full of virtue and determination. Maybe you need to express your belief that they can do a much better job. Maybe you need to get a little more exacting! Perhaps, too, it might mean the development of logical consequences or the suspension of privileges until their duties are done and done well.

The key to begin with is to analyze why the children are behaving as they are, and using reason, prayer, and discussion with them and your husband, see how things can be worked out or made better. The character strengths and weaknesses you notice here can all be transferred or applied to other areas of their lives.

Sloppy bedrooms often mean sloppy grades. Your teaching in a nonthreatening matter such as personal chores has a wider ramification in other areas. Your talks about chores can be easily applied to anything else as well.

Second, aside from what the children are doing, you can keep an eye on how *you* are behaving. Are you being the model of virtue you want to be? How can you improve? Are you being as loving as you want to be? What can you do to change this? Are you as involved in supervising as you need to be? What can you do to improve this?

Third, you might want to assess the children's involvement with God. Are they getting all the grace they need from their own involvement in the Faith? Are you praying for them?

All of these things are ongoing, and you'll need to make time on some regular basis to think and use your reason and discuss with your husband the needs of your children and how you can ensure they're fulfilled.

⁂

In the face of those who would seek to undermine the beauty and dignity of motherhood, or when we ourselves doubt the importance of our mothering and are tempted by discouragement, it would be well to remember something G. K. Chesterton wrote in *What's Wrong With the World?* "How can it be a large career to tell other people's children about the Rule of Three, and a small career to tell one's own children about the universe? How can it be broad to be the same thing to everyone, and narrow to be everything to someone?"

Raising our children is an important job, a "genuine apostolate," and a direct mission from God. All that we do to fulfill our educational responsibilities to our children is *an act of love*. God wants us to do this well. Yes, we need all the help we can get, but we *have* it: God knows that what we're called to do can be so difficult sometimes that we need a special sacrament to have the strength to do it!

He also offers us another help: his own Blessed Mother. Perhaps the most efficacious thing we can do as Catholic mothers is to consecrate ourselves to her, and ask her to love within us, for as Fr. Stefano Gobbi says, *"Mary is Mother. And Mother is the personification of love."*[16]

---

[16] Fr. Eugene Cullinane, *Don Stefano Comes to Combermere* (Combermere, Ontario: Madonna House, c. 1984).

᷍

Chapter 7

The Fifth P: Provider

The fifth P, Provider, involves another aspect of mission to our family: providing for physical needs such as food, clothing, and shelter. It also includes the proper management of our financial resources.

Many times, our responsibilities in this area can overtake some of the higher priorities of family life because our home duties and money concerns are so varied and often time-consuming. Here we want to examine our provider role as God intended it, devote to it the necessary dignity it deserves, yet simultaneously streamline our efforts so that it assumes its rightful place in the five Ps of our vocation. Above all, we need to understand that all our work in the home is good and ordained by God.

The Beauty of Work in the Home

We moved back east from Calgary after two years of marriage and settled on the family farm a couple of miles down the road from Philip's parents. It was lovely. We were surrounded by eighty acres of farmland, and I'd sit at the kitchen table in the morning, staring out the big patio doors at the mist hovering on the fields. Everything seemed so much simpler and quieter there. Yet I faced a hundred new challenges.

The house had to be heated with a wood stove, and I was a bit frightened by the prospect of having a roaring fire in the basement. The only solution was to learn about it, so I studied wood stoves and became quite an expert at running it at exactly the right temperature. We were short on money due to Philip's decreased pay, so I needed to make more things from scratch, bake our own bread, learn to grow a garden and preserve its produce. I began to sew a little bit and got reasonably proficient at it — although my sister-in-law advised me not to quit my "day job" for a career in sewing!

During this new phase of life, I began to see a direct correlation between my efforts and the physical needs of my family. The food I grew in the garden, we picked and ate. The quilts I made by hand kept my kids warm in their beds at night. My work was directly affecting our survival. To be able to do things like this myself was a new challenge. In the past, I guess I had always seen housework and manual labor as things of minimal importance. Housework was something that, as a single woman, I had done quickly on Saturday mornings on my way out of the house to get to bigger and better things. Now I discovered a natural joy came with this manual work, and I found it tremendously motivating to feed my family with the fruit of God's land and my efforts.

We've since moved to a less rural location, and my time is not spent in achieving self-sufficiency as it used to be. But this period in rural Prince Edward Island taught me that manual labor has a dignity and beauty built right into it.

Motherhood Develops Many Skills

I had also believed that the duties of the home were somewhat repetitive and boring and didn't require much skill. Well, working at home with the kids taught me the exact opposite:

home work was more varied, and required as much skill, as any other occupation.

According to the seasons, I was occupied with a great many types of tasks. Spring was planting and cleaning out the house and washing all the bedding and curtains and hanging them out to dry in the fresh spring air. Summer was weeding and beach time and picnics with the kids. Autumn was harvesting and preserving and bundling up the house in preparation for winter. Winter was indoor home improvements and decorating and sewing.

I realized the work I was doing wasn't so very different from jobs out "in the world," and that it often required the application of all the skills, talents, and concentration I could muster. For together with my husband, I was Prime Minister of my home. Every time I organized our family or set up rules or regulations, I was governor. Every time I "arrested" the children for bad behavior, I was the police. Every time I defended my children's rights and arbitrated their squabbles, I was lawyer and judge; and let me tell you, it's no easy thing to decide what is the just and right thing to do when the children are pummeling each other!

I was a teacher when I taught them their ABCs and a priest when I led them in prayer. I was a chef when I cooked their meals and a baker when I made their bread. I was a nutritionist when I planned healthful meals. I was a doctor when I diagnosed ear infections and a nurse when I bandaged a scrape. I was a seamstress, an interior decorator, a manicurist, a janitor, and a toy-maker. I was the manager of my home, and the very process of learning to do and maintain all of this was a skill in itself!

A Custodian of Creation

I later discovered, when I studied Genesis, that my very housework was in a way imaging God's work at creation. In the Garden of Eden, God called man and woman to be stewards of the earth; my share in that stewardship was to care for my home. All my housework was simply the exercise of Christian stewardship over *my* little part of creation.

We are more stewards or custodians of our little pieces of creation than owners, and this applies to our children as well. What we have, be it a little or a lot, has been entrusted to us, for a twofold purpose: to preserve what we have and to administer it profitably. Thus, not only are we to ensure that our home is cared for and kept in order, but we're also called to improve it, to make it meet the real human needs of our family. We don't have the right to neglect our duties here, but are called to manage these resources, for they really belong to God.

I had always found my work in the world easier than my work in the home. But when I came to see myself as a custodian, a manager, then really, I was working for God. This directly affected my attitude about housework. To shirk it was like not to put in a full day's work for a full day's wages — something I never would have done in any employment situation. It was really a matter of justice. So I concluded that to ensure the housework was done and the home and possessions cared for properly was pretty close to a moral obligation.

Dealing with Financial Difficulty

After I left the catechetics position to return home full time, things were tough financially. Philip was working long hours and couldn't really do much more, given that we had small children. If we wanted any family time at all, he couldn't be out working every evening as well as every day.

Philip and I examined what it had cost me to go to work, to buy appropriate clothing, to pay for childcare, to spend more on convenience foods due to lack of cooking time, to cover gas and vehicle maintenance and to buy occasional meals out — not to mention the taxes and deductions from my paycheck. In the end, we figured that my part-time position grossing $1,000 a month netted us in hard cash only about $150! So it didn't really make financial sense to think of going to work again. And practically speaking, with very small children and beginning homeschooling, how much time or energy would I have to work anyway?

So we decided we would keep on as we were, with neither of us taking another job, and do what we could do. But the financial difficulties went on for years. Every time we got on top, something disastrous would happen, and we'd be owing people money again. I remember one autumn we scrimped and saved to pay off all our bills, and by Christmas, we were debt-free. Then the car broke down four times in January and ran up an $800 bill! With no savings, we were in debt again.

This cycle of debt continued to frustrate us. I was upset that the very things I needed to make my home run more smoothly — little things such as new bookshelves, or more storage space, or a better vacuum — were often not financially possible. I'd get mad at God because I felt he had put me in an impossible situation.

So, I figured the only way to deal with it all was to ask myself two questions: "What is up to me?" and "What is up to God?"

Exercising Financial Stewardship

So I had to determine what my responsibilities were, and I came up with a number of things.

First, I had to care properly for what we already possessed. If I found a crayon on the floor, I didn't throw it out; I learned to put it away. I learned to repair things, or better yet, get Philip to! Just before Jessica was born, I spent three months simply fixing all the little things in the house that had broken down, such as replacing some missing floor tiles and repairing our screens.

Next, I realized I could devote my efforts to my home if I couldn't buy much. So I began to make more things from scratch. I grew vegetables in the summer and learned how to pickle and freeze them. And I learned to wallpaper and paint, make my own quilts out of scrap clothing like the early settlers, and sew my own curtains with material at a fraction of the cost of the ready-made drapes. None of this was perfect, but it enabled me to be creative and do some of the things I wanted to do instead of always feeling stifled.

Then, we began to budget and assess more carefully where our money was going. Part of providing for my family meant being financially responsible. Our money was meant to meet the legitimate needs of my family first, as well as aid others less fortunate than we. So I made a list of all our necessary expenses, our debts and bills, and other concerns, and came up with a basic budget to guide me in writing the checks every pay week. Before long, bills began to be paid on time and in full, with less stress.

I also realized that it was because we didn't live by a budget that we never felt that we could purchase what we needed. One little example made this clear to me. I was sitting in the parking lot outside the hardware store. I had wanted a plastic tablecloth cover for more than two years, but because it cost seventeen dollars, I felt that we couldn't afford it. Then it occurred to me that on my many trips to town, I had often spent two dollars here, four dollars there, in little spontaneous spurts. If I had gone into town with a plan, I'd have been able to purchase that plastic cover long before. So, not knowing the state of our finances and not planning for purchases actually led me to *more* impulse spending, almost out of rebellion or frustration, because I felt so powerless to get what I really felt we needed. Once I started planning purchases, the satisfaction of actually buying what I truly wanted helped tame my desires for the stupid little things I used to waste money on.

Distinguishing Between Needs and Wants

Part of financial stewardship also involves not just avoiding frivolous spending, but recognizing that all we have has been entrusted to us so that we may fulfill our mission to raise our children and even to help those less fortunate than we. This means that we need to distinguish between our essential needs and our excessive wants. For often, rich or poor, we just want *more*.

One day I was pining away for some new pregnancy clothes. I was tired of the ten outfits I had in my closet, and I wanted some new ones. I hopped in the car that weekend, drove a fair way to the only pregnancy boutique on my side of the island, and searched for a new wardrobe. After I had made a few purchases (with money my mother had sent me out of pity), I sat in my car and felt slightly guilty. I sat there pondering why, and then it struck me: I didn't *really* need these clothes; I just *wanted* them. By gosh, I was suffering from greed, not need! I had plenty of clothes back home, all in good repair. With only a couple of months of pregnancy left, surely I could have held out. But no. I had acted on a desire for *things* for their own sake.

Then I knew: *I simply had to stop wanting so much stuff.* My desires and expectations more reflected our affluent and consumerist culture than any real needs of my family. Seeing as how we so often struggled financially, I began to look at my lifestyle and assess which expenses came from the legitimate needs of my family and which came merely from wants.

Of course, it's not wrong simply to want some nice things. But there's always a danger that our attitude toward possessions can become a problem: when I desire things to the point of resentment toward God or jealousy toward those who have more than I; when I go into debt to buy more unnecessary things; when I seek wants at the expense of supplying what my family needs, thus compromising my family's overall financial picture without good reason; when I seek my personal fulfillment in possessions instead of in God; or when I can't control my desires for material goods and deprive myself the practice of Christian mortification.

Just as we have a mission to love our husbands and children, so, too, we have a mission with our goods: they're meant to meet the needs of our families and to help those around us in need. We have a serious duty to help others with our resources in some way. "In his use of things man should regard the external things he legitimately owns not merely as exclusive to himself but common to others also, in the sense that they can benefit others as well as himself."[17] *We do not have the right to keep for our exclusive use what we do not need when others lack necessities.*[18]

I read a long time ago something St. Thomas Aquinas said about using money solely for our own benefit: that by pampering ourselves, we superficially shelter ourselves from the realities of life, so when serious difficulties come, we're unprepared spiritually to cope with them. Affluence, which is a superfluous abundance of goods, can actually harm our characters and weaken our spiritual lives if used improperly. And Jesus himself warned us that we can't serve two masters.[19]

---

[17] CCC, par. 2404.

[18] John A. Hardon, S.J., *The Catholic Catechism* (Garden City, New York: Doubleday and Company, Inc., 1975), 388.

[19] Matt. 6:24.

Gaining Financial Perspective

So Philip and I continued to struggle with financial matters, and with the often-strong desires to want more and buy more. Deep down I knew that if I were rich, I probably would just randomly buy everything I wanted anyway, and perhaps God knew that I would suffer spiritual consequences as a result.

Nevertheless, knowing all this didn't make it any easier. After all, I couldn't instantly change my own heart. I just wanted all the beautiful stuff and modern conveniences I knew the world could offer me. Since they were there, why couldn't I have them? And sometimes I'd get mad at God.

One day, I made a large poster with pictures of children and families from all over the world that I'd cut out of *National Geographic* magazines, laminated it, and hung it in my kitchen. When I'd get frustrated because I couldn't buy what I wanted, I'd go and sit desolately in front of that poster.

I'd see the African man carrying on his shoulder the large loaf of bread that he'd gotten from the Christian mission as he walked for miles to bring it to his family; and I'd remember the twenty bags of groceries I had just brought home, with bread, yes, but also with peanut butter and Cheese Whiz and meats and maple syrup and chocolate chips. . . .

I'd look at the pictures of the Asian family who sat around outside on rocks by an open fire on a frosty morning, shivering, while I sat in my snugly warm house with my steaming cup of coffee and warm toast and jam.

I'd see the woman who cooked in a hole in her wall, with some wood and a grate, or the family who sat on International Aid grain buckets for their furniture; and I'd look around at my electric stove and fridge and dishwasher and comfy upholstered couches and chairs.

And I'd see Romanian children gathered on dirty old carpets in a bare room, plaster peeling off the walls by the broken window, sitting around an old man with a single book as he gave them their lessons. And I'd think about my bookshelves full of books and drawers full of notebooks and my globe and educational videos and my chalkboard and my desks and art supplies and computer.

I'd see the picture of the little boy, a patch over a damaged eye, his face ravaged by shrapnel and the pain of war, and compare it with the glistening eyes and rosy cheeks of my children who knew no more than sibling rivalry. And I'd say to myself, "Why them? Why me?" And I couldn't come up with any answers, except that I had a great many blessings and a tremendous responsibility to be grateful for what I had. And I'd have to get up and say to God, "I'm sorry. Thank you. Help me," and go do my dishes.

Living Within Our Means

The key to fulfilling our stewardship role is that it's the Lord who provides, and we're called to work within the resources he makes available to us. We must live within our means, whether we've been graced with abundance or with deficit.

For those who suffer want in a little way or in a great way, we must fully commit to do our part in trying to meet the needs of our family. But in doing so, if we still find ourselves with financial difficulties, we don't have to ignore all our other priorities in search of money or allow anxiety to build within us. Instead we just need to trust in God and his promises a little more, become a bit more discerning about essential needs and excessive wants, a bit more frugal than the Joneses next door might have to be, and guard our hearts against jealousy of the rich and bitterness about our lack.

In addition, there may be a point in our lives when we're called to a little more asceticism than others around us. If we're doing our utmost to manage God's resources well, there's no reason to see financial difficulties as something outside of God's permitting will, or something that his providence will not make up for. "The art of being poor is to trust God for everything, to demand nothing — and to be grateful for all that is given."[20]

On the other hand, there are those of us who suffer not from deficits, but from the burden of abundance. In this instance, God has called us to an expansion of our provider role, including not only our family, but the greater society as well. "[God] gives to some people more than they need, not [so] that they can enjoy great luxury, but to make them stewards on behalf of orphans, the sick, and the crippled."[21]

If we've been blessed with the responsibility of much, we owe it to the poor and to God to manage it as responsibly as possible and place our resources at the service of the larger society.

The Necessity of Tithing

Still asking myself "What can I do?" about our financial situation, a careful reading of the *Catechism* and Scripture eventually convinced me that tithing was an obligation for Philip and me. Scripture says that not paying the tithe is actually to rob God!

> From the days of your fathers, you have turned aside from my statutes and have not kept them. Return to me, and I will return to you, says the Lord of hosts. But you say, "How shall we return?" Will man rob God? Yet you are robbing me. But you say, "How are we robbing thee?" In your tithes

---

[20] St. John Chrysostom, *On Living Simply: The Golden Voice of John Chrysostom*, comp. Robert Van de Weyer. (Liguori, Missouri: Liguori / Triumph Publications, 1996), 7.

[21] Ibid., 6.

and offerings. You are cursed with a curse, for you are robbing me; the whole nation of you. Bring the full tithes into the storehouse, that there may be food in my house; and thereby put me to the test, says the Lord of hosts, if I will not open the windows of Heaven for you and pour down for you an overflowing blessing. I will rebuke the devourer for you, so that it will not destroy the fruits of your soil; and your vine in the field shall not fail to bear, says the Lord of hosts. Then all nations will call you blessed, for you will be a land of delight, says the Lord of hosts.[22]

And this answered the second question I had asked about financial responsibilities: "What is up to God?" God was telling me to trust him — that I could "test" him on this and that I would not be outdone in generosity. Not only would he actively and adequately provide, but he would prevent unforeseen circumstances from preventing the fulfillment of our provider role.

God Provides

Now, Philip and I had tithed before, but it had often been an on-again, off-again sort of thing. If we ran into financial difficulties, sometimes there seemed to be a real excuse to stop tithing or to reduce the tithe, and it became very hard to resume. But most often I found myself reluctant to tithe when we *had* the adequate resources we needed! It was *then* that I'd get mad at God for taking all "our" money, forgetting completely that all belongs to God and I'm only the steward. At other times, we'd grit our teeth, stick with it, and would experience very definite blessings. It wasn't uncommon at these times for me to say ,"Okay, Lord, I need a check in the

[22] Mal. 3:7-12.

mail on Monday morning," and sure enough, one would be wait-ing for me in the mailbox. I remember one three-month period when we had over $800 come in from unexpected sources every single month.

Another memorable time, our tithing and other expenses seemed to be running us into the ground. Our monthly budget was putting us $400 in the hole every month. I took it to a friend who was good with figures and asked him what we could do. "I honestly don't know," he said, shaking his head in wonder. Philip and I de-cided to carry on. Within three months, our situation had totally turned around. We had a "money miracle," paid off our debts, and the budget problems were reversed.

Not that we *counted* on money miracles, mind you, although we've had plenty. But when people tithe, as a matter of justice, God intervenes in many ways to help provide for his children: by revealing to us financial planning ideas that we hadn't thought of before; by leading us to a particular store with sales on many of the grocery items we need for the week; by bringing about new em-ployment opportunities when the present job isn't meeting our needs; by coincidental gifts from others; and by sending unex-pected checks in the mail. Philip once got a refund on a speeding ticket from a province on the opposite coast of Canada ten years after the fact — and just in time to pay a bill! The point is that *God provides*, intervening in time and space to help his children by one means or another, even if it does take a miracle.

A Significant Blessing of Tithing

Despite the many interventions I experienced when we tithed, it still took a long while to believe God, and our financial state fluctuated in accordance with our trust. Whenever we stopped tithing, things would quickly degenerate.

In the end, I learned something very significant about tithing: it's a tool, a means to detach our hearts from inordinate desires. Whereas before I would sit desolate in front of my poster and resign myself with sinking heart to doing without, after the commitment to tithing was established, my very desires began to change. Tithing was an entryway for the grace of God to change my heart, that very same heart that I can't change on my own. Where once I couldn't get enough of homeschooling books, suddenly I felt a desire to be free of too much curriculum and to simplify. Where once everything in my house seemed old and ugly, now I was comfortable and happy and grateful for what we had.

Thus, tithing is not only a means of giving God what belongs to him and exercising self-control, but is actually a real channel of grace to enable us to be satisfied with having our needs met, with a few little wants thrown in as gifts from the goodness of God.

Just as God's provision of the earth was meant to meet the human needs of Adam and Eve, and, in doing so, he provided a paradise, so, too, my home needed to meet a twofold purpose: it had to be *functional* and beautiful, at least to us. Therefore, each room was meant to serve a specific purpose, and it was meant to be arranged and supplied with what was necessary to fulfill its purpose.

That meant it had to be set up properly. I began by doing what I called a "room analysis." I walked around from room to room with a clipboard and asked myself some questions.

What is the purpose of this room, and what does it need for that purpose? I wanted my children's rooms to be places where they not only slept and stored their clothing, but also where they did things such as read and draw and play; so I wrote down all those activities. Then, beside each activity I wrote down what they needed to have in the room to do it. To read, they had to have a table for their books and lamps. They needed some drawers to store drawing materials, they needed paper and crayons and pencils and erasers, and they needed a toy box; plus, of course, their beds and their dressers. If I want the family to pray in the living room, I needed to make a specific place there for the storage of rosaries and prayer books.

I did this for each room in the house. There was no point in putting school books in the kitchen if I used a classroom. If I needed my cookbooks in the kitchen, perhaps I should put a shelf in there instead of storing them in the living room. There was no reason why everything couldn't be in a permanent place chosen *because that was where it was most typically used*. I later realized this helped my children know exactly where to put things back. They can't help keep things tidy if there isn't a logical and set place for things.

Next I had to determine whether anything needed to be removed. *What shouldn't stay in this room?* Since I had additional storage space, I didn't need to store their summer roller blades in the bedroom, nor any summer clothes during the winter. So I moved these things out of their rooms. If my porch was meant just for coats and hats and mitts and boots and keys and purses, then I took out the garbage cans and toys from this area because they didn't belong there. I set up a "transfer room" where I could temporarily store stuff while I was getting the other rooms in order. Then I tackled that room last.

While I was at it, I examined each room to see whether any repairs needed to be done. I wrote these all down on a repair list and put a big star beside things that were urgent. Some items have ended up sitting on my list for years. If something breaks, I just go to this list, which I keep in a notebook, and add on. Then, when

I'm budgeting, I can go to this list to see what needs to be done next. I never need to remember all this in my head, because it's on paper.

While I was at it, I also wrote down any beautifying projects I wanted to accomplish. *What improvements would I like to make to this room?* Many of these things remain undone on my list, too, but many have also been tackled.

Before leaving each room, I thought I might as well figure out what it needed to be kept clean. *What chores need to be done in this room?* And so I wrote down exactly what chores were absolutely required to maintain tidiness and order on a daily, weekly, or seasonal basis. To me, making beds and putting away clothes, books, and toys were necessary daily duties in the bedrooms. Tidying drawers, vacuuming, and dusting were things I could reserve for every two weeks in the bedrooms, along with a sheet change. Twice a year, we'd do a good cleaning together and wash down whatever was dirty, sort and store seasonal clothing, and wash the blankets and curtains.

But there was something else. *Who was going to do each of these chores?* I've never believed that all the work in the home is Mummy's job. Good managers don't do every little thing themselves. Instead, they delegate jobs to each according to capacity. And as a friend of mine once said, "When kids can ride skateboards and bicycles, they can certainly learn how to wield a vacuum cleaner!" Children and husband are not called to do chores just to "help Mummy." They're called to be stewards over their little part of creation, too, just as I am.

So, for every chore of every room, daily, weekly, and seasonal, I went through the list and decided who was capable of doing what. There was something for everyone, guaranteed! So I made up chore charts and posted them in the appropriate places. Weekly downstairs cleaning charts went in the kitchen. Bedroom tidy-up was posted in each room.

And so the next question became, *when were these chores going to be done?* I placed bedroom chores around getting-up and going-to-bed times. I scheduled kitchen chores and most downstairs tidy-up chores before and after meal times. We cleaned the downstairs once a week on Friday, followed that evening by a "motivating factor" of pop, hot dogs, chips, and a video. Upstairs cleaning was every second Saturday, followed by the rest of the day off. For seasonal chores, I just planned on a couple of weeks in the spring and the fall to get done what was on my list. Laundry I placed in optional time frames, before and after breakfast, during the kids' recesses, when I began supper, and so forth. So whenever I had spare moments, I'd do a load. The kids would return it to their rooms before lunch or supper and put it away before bedtime.

Other chores that popped up, such as feeding the cats and getting the garbage out, I just wrote down whenever I realized they weren't accounted for and set a time for them to be done.

I also sat down with my husband and helped him go through a home-and-property analysis that dealt with the needs outside the house as well — the lawns, garage, shed, garden, and so on. Then we added any chores and kept the lists of repairs, purchases, and projects for future reference.

Working Out Your Essentials

The first thing to do is get your home in order and work out your chore routines. You might want to turn to other resources for help. I've read a lot of home-management books, and all of them have something to offer. Almost any program you're attracted to will suffice, but I do recommend the process just explained because it's so simple.

When you're done with that and things are flowing fairly smoothly, you'll want to look at pulling together your finances and budgeting, if you or your husband aren't already doing so. Again, there are numerous resources available to help you, but here I can offer a simple one to get you started.

First, discuss this with your husband and work on it together as much as possible. Which of you is more suited to manage the finances? Would it be helpful to hire someone else better suited to the task?

Then, purchase a filing cabinet and some files, or clean out the one you already have. Make a folder for every important paper you have in your entire house. File it in alphabetical order. Make room for receipts you'll now be saving, and get one book to record your expenses and another for weekly, biweekly, or monthly budgeting. Set up a day every week or every two weeks or every month when you'll do the books and plan purchases.

Next, sit down with prior records or receipts, or make an educated estimate about the following:

- *How much income do we have coming in on a regular basis?*

- *How much are we required to tithe in order to ensure we meet this obligation and experience God's blessings?*

- *What are our basic and necessary monthly expenses?* Consider mortgage or rent, insurance costs, vehicles heating, cooling, bank charges, electricity, gas, vehicle payments, phone, Internet, groceries, vehicle repairs, medical and dental expenses, clothing, yearly dues (vehicle registration, sewer costs, licenses, taxes), and so on.

- *How much money do we owe, aside from car and home payments? Whom do we owe? How much? What are the payment schedules?*

• *What other expenses do we normally incur? What would be an average monthly or yearly total on these (home maintenance, clothing, education, and so on)?*

• *At this time, can we allot anything to savings, no matter how small? If not, why is this? Is there anything we can do to begin saving regularly? If we have a lot left, is there some special way we can help those less fortunate than we? Are there any debts we could apply this to in order to pay them off sooner?*

Based on the figures you've come up with, work out a monthly budget with your husband including tithing, necessary expenses, and debt reduction as the first priority. Include also some small sum of "personal money" that each of you is free to spend to avoid total frustration.

Beyond the Basics

Because our Provider role takes up so much of our time, it will take some time to get all of this in order. It wouldn't be unreasonable for it to take a year or more to pull it all together. The key is to work at it consistently and begin somewhere.

As you go, the heart of the Rule in this area is something you can ponder during your prayer times and personal space days. God is very interested in helping you pull all this together, as he knows it will significantly reduce any stress you've been undergoing — and he wants you happy and healthy!

Reflect on whether you really see your Provider role as a stewardship mission to be shared with God, or as something that falls totally on your shoulders. To take all the responsibility for your home and finances can often cause serious stress and hopelessness if there are difficulties. Are there any ways you need to foster trust in God?

Are there things you could do to take better care of what you do have? Is there much waste going on in relation to things, clothing, or electricity? Can you do more things yourself to help save money? Are there things you need to hire help for in order to make room for other greater priorities in your life?

Are you suffering from greediness instead of neediness? What can you do to curb inordinate desires for stuff? Are you thanking God for the good things He has provided? If you are in need of more income, is there any way you can apply your talents and interests in a reasonable way to help meet these needs?

≈

With the fifth P, Provider, we complete the specific aspects of the married vocation. The heart of this priority is to recognize clearly that even the most mundane work has a high dignity placed upon it by God, and that all we do with our possessions and money is meant to fulfill the stewardship responsibilities God has called us to.

We can be tempted to let this priority override all the others, being so consumed with housework or employment that we let the people in our life slide by the wayside. But really, the fifth P is really just about providing an orderly stage upon which all the drama of loving relationships must occur; we want the actors to focus on the performance, not on a messy, disorganized set.

We need to streamline all our duties in this sphere, so that we can truly have time to attend to our relationship with God, our husbands, and our children in a loving and recollected way.

Chapter 8

⌒

Pulling Together Your Rule

At this point, you've completed a basic analysis of all the major aspects of your vocation, and I've given you suggestions for schedules and charts to account for each of the five Ps. By now, you may have a general idea of some of the time frames in which you want to do things. You may even be implementing them already, and need to do only a little finishing work.

But perhaps you're looking at a notebook full of scribbles and feel in need of a little more direction to help pull it all together. So here I'll walk you through the scheduling and charting method I used when I created my Rule. I'll help you create a basic schedule divided into daily, weekly, and seasonal sections. It won't account for *all* your possibilities, but it will get you started. You can refer to my complete Rule and samples of other charts elsewhere in this book to help you visualize what the finished product could look like.

Going through this process can seem daunting at times, especially if you read this chapter through in one sitting! However, in the end, you'll have your entire Rule and all the necessary work details broken down into a few pieces of paper or poster board posted around your house. You'll never need to go through this detailed analysis again! And, in fact, eventually, you won't even need to refer to them again, nor will your children, because it will all become a habit. The charts and written schedules are training tools to help you know what to do when, and to help you get into the routine of managing your life and growing closer to God all at the same time.

Establishing Daily Time Frames

First we will establish a basic framework for your daily schedule. (Refer to Table 1.)

On a piece of paper or two (or ten!), you'll begin your rough copy. Divide your page into as many vertical columns as there are people in your family. Now make large horizontal rows, and fill in a time on the left margin of each row, beginning with the time you've decided to get out of bed, and carrying on with half-hour (or quarter-hour) increments until your established bedtime. Then, in the proper box, enter "Get up" and "Bedtime." Do the same for each of your children's columns.

Next, refer to your daily prayer routine, and in your column write "Prayer" in those time slots you've decided to devote to prayer. Then fill in the activities you've determined the children will be doing at each of your personal prayer times. If they're to join you at certain prayer times, fill this in under their names as well. If you have different things planned for different days, either for yourself or for the children, differentiate the activities in the same time slot; for example: "M/T/F Mass, W/Th/Sa Scripture." Include family prayer time and if you've arranged with your children their own separate prayer times, write these in the appropriate boxes as well.

The next most natural time slots can be assigned to meals. Enter breakfast, lunch, and dinner in the appropriate time boxes (and any snack times if you have little ones). I usually enter these in large print across all the columns in that row, for we all do these things at the same time.

Enter any other natural breaks, such as children's recess or outside time, covering as many columns in that row as applies to the number of children doing it. If you work outside the home, include driving times, dropping off children, coffee breaks, and lunch hours. Include here as well nap times for the little ones, filling in under the child's name the boxes equaling the time they normally sleep. In addition, if there are things you need to specifically do for your husband, and can do it at a set time on a regular basis, enter these, too.

Scheduling a Time for Daily Chores

Next, we want to set times for all the chores that need to be accomplished in the run of a normal day. (Refer to Table 2.)

Begin with hygiene tasks. Assuming a morning and evening necessity for these, enter into the appropriate boxes "Morning chores — hygiene," and "Evening chores — hygiene." Personal morning tasks can follow upon rising and be included in the "Get up" box, or they can follow breakfast. Evening tasks can be allotted to the box right before bed, or even right after supper for little ones. Enter these tasks for each of your children in the appropriate boxes.

Next, the simplest thing to do is to attach kitchen and other chores to the mealtimes. For example, you can establish pre-breakfast and post-breakfast chores. You can choose to place these into other time frames as well, depending on your circumstances. That's up to you; this is just a simplified method to get you started. For each meal, then, allot a space for the "pre" and "post" chores and write them in the appropriate boxes.

Table 1: Daily Time Frames

	Mummy	Anna	Nicki	Jessi	Luke	Virginia
6:30	Wake up	Sleeping				
7:00	Morning prayer					
7:30		Wake up				
8:00	BREAKFAST					
8:30						
9:00	MORNING FAMILY PRAYER					
9:30						
10:00	Midmorning prayer	Outdoor recess				
10:30						
11:00						
11:30						
12:00	LUNCH					
12:30						
1:00	Midday prayer	Quiet time in rooms				
1:30						
2:00						
2:30						
3:00						
3:30	Coffee break	Outdoor recess				
4:00						
4:30						
5:00						
5:30	SUPPER					
6:00						
6:30						
7:00						
7:30	EVENING FAMILY PRAYER					
8:00					Bedtime	
8:30			Bedtime			
9:00		Bedtime				
9:30		Sleeping				
10:00	Evening prayer					
10:30	Bedtime					

Table 2: Daily Chore Times

	Mummy	Anna	Nicki	Jessi	Luke	Virginia
6:30	Wake up	Sleeping				
7:00	Morning prayer					
7:30	Morning chores — hygiene — pre-breakfast chores					
8:00	BREAKFAST					
8:30	Post-breakfast chores					
9:00	MORNING FAMILY PRAYER					
9:30						
10:00	Midmorning prayer	Outdoor recess				
10:30						
11:00						
11:30	Pre-lunch chores					
12:00	LUNCH					
12:30	Post-lunch chores					
1:00	Midday prayer	Quiet time in rooms				
1:30						
2:00						
2:30						
3:00						
3:30	Coffee break	Outdoor recess				
4:00						
4:30	Pre-supper chores					
5:00		Pre-supper chores				
5:30		SUPPER				
6:00		Post-supper chores				
6:30						
7:00		Evening chores — hygiene				
7:30	EVENING FAMILY PRAYER					
8:00		Dog care	Free		Bedtime	
8:30		Free	Bedtime			
9:00		Bedtime				
9:30	Evening chores	Sleeping				
10:00	Evening prayer					
10:30	Bedtime					

You may also want to include another time for chores. I have an "Evening chores" time scheduled for later in the evening that pertains to things I need to do to tidy or prep for the next day.

Developing Daily Routine Charts

At this point, you've scheduled your rising times and bedtimes, your daily prayer, hygiene, meal, and chore times, and other miscellaneous daily occurrences. Now we want to itemize these on separate charts and post them in a logical place. I suggest you do a rough chart for each category initially, and over the following week or two, insert things you forgot to include in your analysis. After a while, unexpected things will stop popping up, and you can make more permanent charts. Eventually you might even want to laminate them: a lot of sticky little fingers will be handling these charts, as every member of your family will refer to them.

For your prayer times, make a small chart including which prayer forms you decided to do in each time slot. (Refer to Table 3A.) Since these charts can be reviewed regularly, you might also want to include on this chart any faith-study topics you want to do for the following year. This chart can be placed in your prayer spot, perhaps between the pages of your Bible, for easy reference when you go to pray.

Next, make two charts called "Morning Chores" and "Evening Chores." (Refer to Table 3B.) These will be done in the hygiene time slots you've allotted. Here refer to your notebook, scanning for all the tasks that you and your children need to do in these time frames. For morning chores, list, or draw, the duties everyone has to do, regardless of age: "Hygiene: wash face and hands, brush teeth and hair, get dressed." "Bedrooms: make beds, put away pajamas, tidy bedroom." Be specific, and include every chore.

Table 3A: Prayer Options

Morning prayer (30 minutes)	Divine Office: Morning Prayer (with Philip if possible) and formal prayers, Morning Offering and/or quiet or journaling
Morning family prayer (15 minutes)	Formal prayers and Morning Offering and hymns or saint story or Catechism story or Bible story or spiritual or virtue teaching
Midmorning prayer (15 minutes)	Divine Mercy Chaplet or Scripture meditation or Divine Office: Midmorning Prayer
Midday prayer/quiet (1 hour)	Divine Office: Midday Psalmody and Office of Readings and spiritual reading or Scripture or quiet or journaling
Afternoon coffee break	Divine Office: Midafternoon Prayer
Evening family prayer (20 minutes)	Rosary or Divine Mercy Chaplet or short prayers (occasional hymns or faith stories)
Evening prayer (20 minutes)	Divine Office: Night Prayer (with Philip if possible)
Spiritual reading	This year: Teresa of Avila's and Hubert Van Zeller's works; Fr. Thomas Dubay's *Fire Within*
Faith-study topics	This year: *Old Testament*; sacramental aspect of marriage; *Catholic Catechism*
Miscellaneous	

Table 3B: Morning and Evening Chores

MORNING CHORES					
Mummy	Anna	Nicki	Jessi	Luke	Virginia
Wash face and hands (Hang up face cloth and towel) Brush teeth and hair (Put away brushes; cap toothpaste) Get dressed and put pajamas away Quick bedroom tidying — books, toys, clothes, garbage Make bed					
	Care for dog	Take laundry downstairs and return basket to upstairs	Help Virginia to do the above chores	Turn off upstairs lights and bring down any dishes from upstairs	Do what Jessi tells you

EVENING CHORES					
Mummy	Anna	Nicki	Jessi	Luke	Virginia
Set up coffee maker Quick downstairs tidying up Unload/load dishwasher Set breakfast table Put Philip's and my laundry away Shower (or wait until morning) Feed cats Check calendar and weekly schedule to get an idea of tomorrow	Bath or shower, depending on the day (Ask Mummy) Wash face and hands (Hang up face cloth and towel) Brush teeth and hair (Put away brushes; cap toothpaste) Put on pajamas Put dirty clothes in upstairs laundry basket Put own clean laundry away Quick bedroom tidying — books, toys, clothes, garbage				

Then move into the duties that are done by specific people, and divide your chart into columns with a name at the top of each. Record the specific chore to be done by each person under his or her name. This can include any other things that pop up as you go along; at a later date, I entered under specific names things such as bringing down the laundry (Nicki), and turning out the upstairs lights (Luke), bringing down any dishes that had migrated to bedrooms (Luke), helping Virginia fulfill her morning chores of hygiene, dressing, and bed-making (Jessica), and letting the dog out for his morning necessities (Anna). Post this chart in a logical place (mine was in the upstairs hall), and fill in a chart for the evening chores along the same line.

You'll want to account for your evening chores here as well. I've posted a little list of things I need to do before I go to bed. These usually take me about half an hour.

Next, work out your pre- and post-meal chore charts. (Refer to Tables 4A, 4B, and 4C). Start with rough copies. On three pieces of paper, write the specific meal in the middle of the paper in big letters. Now you have a section above it for pre-meal chores and a section below it for post-meal chores. Make as many vertical columns on each page as you have people involved, and label each column with a person's name.

Begin with your actual meal chores. What tasks need to be done before the meal (setting the table, cooking)? Which ones need to be done after (cleaning off the table, washing the dishes)? Who is capable of doing each? Enter each task under an appropriate name and in the proper time slot.

Now we can expand a bit upon what will happen in these chore times. Were there any other chores you wanted done on a daily basis that can be fit in here, such as tidying up each of the rooms, getting out the vitamins, sweeping, straightening up the shoes and boots and mitts, feeding the dog, and so forth? Scan your notebook for *all* the daily chores and parcel these out according to ability and availability.

You'll need to juggle to create a balanced, even work schedule for each person. You can also juggle tasks between different meal times; you might find that you've overloaded breakfast chores and have little to do at lunch or supper. Here, you can assess which chores can be done at a better time to even out the work during the day.

Include laundry routines here as well. I usually just write "Laundry" under my column for every pre- and post-chore time and in other little sections throughout my day. (Having it written down regularly helps me remember.) I schedule the children to take the laundry upstairs before supper.

You'll find that things pop up as you go. Again, keep your charts in a rough form for a couple of weeks, and when something arises, go to the charts and ask yourself, "Who can do it?" and "When can it be done?" and enter the answers.

After a few weeks, you can make a good copy of your meal chart; I usually have one chart with all the meal routines on it. Laminate it, and post it in the kitchen somewhere. Keep these same tasks for at least one year. Soon everyone will develop habits, and your charts won't be used as much.

Scheduling Other Daily Constants

So far, we've covered prayer as well as all the major chores that must be done daily, including personal-hygiene tasks, tidying and other daily housecleaning activities, meals and kitchen cleanup, as well as things you might need to do for your husband. This routine alone will keep you fed and rested, your children and your

Table 4A: Breakfast Chores

Mummy	Anna	Nicki	Jessi	Luke	Virginia
Help with breakfast and set table if needed Unload dishwasher Do laundry	Feed dog Make breakfast	Make breakfast for self and help Luke	Vitamins to all kids Make own and Virginia's breakfast	Make breakfast for self or get Nicki's help	
SAY GRACE EAT BREAKFAST					
Take own dishes to sink					
Do laundry Load dishes Wipe counter School prep Misc. & tidy		Compost, waste, and recycling emptied	Sweep kitchen	Wipe table Flowers on table	Hang towels

Table 4B: Lunch Chores

Mummy	Anna	Nicki	Jessi	Luke	Virginia
Make lunch Do laundry Set table	Care for dog Help with lunch	Tidy classroom Help Luke	Tidy living room	Tidy porch Tidy mittens and boots	Help set table
		SAY GRACE EAT LUNCH			
Make coffee Load dishes Do laundry Brush teeth	Feed dog Settle Luke and Virginia for quiet time Brush teeth	Clear table Wipe table Brush teeth	Sweep kitchen Brush teeth and help Virginia with teeth	Tidy chairs and flowers Brush teeth	Tidy towels Brush teeth

Table 4C: Supper Chores

Mummy	Anna	Nicki	Jessi	Luke	Virginia
Laundry Baking Dishwasher Make supper Set table Phone calls	Tidy living room Put laundry away	Tidy classroom Put laundry away	Tidy porch Put laundry away	Tidy hall and stairs	Tidy mittens and boots
		Put own laundry away			
	SAY GRACE EAT SUPPER				
Sweep downstairs	Clean kitchen: clear and wipe table; load and run dishwasher; sweep; tidy and wash counters; towels; chairs; flowers				

clothes clean, your rooms tidy, and your spiritual life in order. This is a significant feat, really!

But now you'll find that you're getting into things specific to your own circumstances, and what I do may not be applicable. What you'll notice, if you've followed my method, is that there are now large chunks of time, between meals and in the evening, when you don't have anything scheduled yet. Here you need to determine how you're going to use that time.

I spend my mornings and a good portion of the afternoon homeschooling. The time slots on my schedule just say "School." But I have another schedule I follow on another chart, with the time and tasks divided up according to person, just as with the main schedule. And while I list a general progression of events, and use multiperson scheduling to permit some children to do one thing while I do another, I use this school schedule more flexibly. It's often different from day to day, which cuts back on monotony, and I often change it from time to time to account for the seasons and the level of cabin fever we experience. The key here is that, from about 9:00 a.m. to noon, aside from a recess and prayer break, we have school. That is all my Rule is concerned with.

In the afternoons, after time with the kids, I usually have a time set aside for other work. This can be anything — from special home projects to regular weekly chores (which we'll get to in a moment), to visits or gardening or baking or whatever. The key here is that every afternoon I can expect to be doing something with that time, and it's usually planned the night before or near the end of my quiet time after lunch.

In the evenings, I set aside time for a walk (although I'm not as faithful to it as I should be!). I have a time set aside for personal hobbies, other recreation, or free time with the kids. Most of the evening after the kids' bedtime is set aside for my husband first or for study projects or sewing tasks or anything I can do in a leisurely, relaxing fashion.

You may have outside employment scheduled in these available time frames, or special activities you do with your children, or a home business you attend to, or whatever. *Routinize* everything you can. Set aside a chunk of time for your remaining daily duties, whatever they may be, and do them in the time frame allotted. (Refer to Table 5 for my completed daily schedule.)

Organizing Your Weekly and Seasonal Schedules

There are many things that don't happen on a daily basis, but happen weekly or biweekly, and still other things that happen only on a seasonal basis. We want to simplify these, too, as much as possible.

First, I suggest drawing up a small chart titled "Weekly Routines." Set it up for two weeks, or even for four weeks, reflecting a monthly calendar, listing all the days and dividing each day up into three sections: morning, afternoon, and evening. (Refer to Tables 6A and 6B.) Now enter things that happen only every week, or every other week, or even monthly. For this, go through your notebook, and pick out each thing you had planned to do that didn't fall within a daily routine, and enter it on the appropriate day, in the appropriate time frame.

Start with your personal needs and those of your family. These can include spiritual needs: prayer groups, Adoration hours, Mass and Confession, retreat days and spiritual direction, or catechism classes. Include also hobbies and exercise and social events for you and your children: painting classes, skating lessons, a trip to the gym or the pool, a night out with friends, scheduled visits to Grandma's. Allot a place for any regular activities you do with your husband, such as a night out, or those things that he or you

Table 5: Completed Daily Schedule

	Mummy	Anna	Nicki	Jessi	Luke	Virginia
6:30	Wake up	Sleeping				
7:00	Prayer/laundry					
7:30	Morning chores — hygiene — pre-breakfast chores					
8:00	BREAKFAST					
8:30	Post-breakfast chores					
9:00	MORNING FAMILY PRAYER (Mass on Mon/Tues/Fri)					
9:30	School					
10:00	Midmorning prayer	Outdoor recess (dog outside, too!)				
10:30	School					
11:00						
11:30	Pre-lunch chores					
12:00	LUNCH					
12:30	Post-lunch chores					
1:00	Prayer/laundry	Quiet time in rooms				
1:30	School					
2:00						
2:30						
3:00						
3:30	Coffee /laundry	Outdoor recess (dog outside, too!)				
4:00	Pre-supper chores	Older children play with younger ones				
4:30						
5:00		Pre-supper chores				
5:30		SUPPER				
6:00	Free: walk, recreation, fun, hobbies	Post-supper chores				
6:30		Free Time				
7:00		Evening Chores — hygiene				
7:30	EVENING FAMILY PRAYER					
8:00	Philip, weekly events, sewing, miscellaneous, study, hobbies	Dog	Free	Free	Bedtime	
8:30		Free	Bedtime			
9:00		Bedtime				
9:30	Evening chores	Sleeping				
10:00	Evening prayer					
10:30	Bedtime					

Table 6A: Weekly Routines (Week 1)

	Sunday	Monday	Tuesday	Wednesday	Thursday	Friday	Saturday
Morning	Music ministry at Mass (9:00)	Adoration (5:00) Mass (9:00)	Mass (9:00) Waste collection	Defrost and clean fridge and freezer		Mass (9:00) Every third week recyclables get collected	Clean upstairs Change sheets Clean toothbrushes
Afternoon	Manicures: kids and I			Week A: My kids to Heidi's Week B: Heidi's kids here		Kids visit their aunt Errands and appointments	Kids visit Grandma Kids' confessions (once a month)
Evening	Plan week	Catechism classes: Dad and kids (6:30)		Bible study	Finances	Clean downstairs (4:00 or 5:00) Adoration (11:00)	Phil and I: date!

Table 6B: Weekly Routines (Week II)

	Sunday	Monday	Tuesday	Wednesday	Thursday	Friday	Saturday
Morning	Music ministry at Mass (9:00)	Adoration (5:00) Mass (9:00)	Mass (9:00) Compost collection		Payday!	Mass (9:00) Every third week recyclables get collected	Mummy's day out
Afternoon	Manicures: kids and I			Visit Grandma (1:30).		Cousins visit us	Mummy's day out Confession Groceries
Evening	Plan week	Catechism classes: Phillip and kids (6:30)	Music ministry practice (7:00)	Bible study	Finances Groceries now or Saturday	Clean downstairs (4:00 or 5:00) Adoration (11:00)	Phil and I: date!

wish to do regularly, such as a volunteer activity. Include other personal things that happen only once a week or less often, such as getting a manicure or getting your hair done.

Look here to the weekly and monthly chores you noted when you did your room analysis. Set up a time for these as well: the weekly clean, garbage days, washing bedding and towels, cleaning the fridge or oven, and so on. Include other things as well, such as time for doing your finances, paying bills and balancing the books, buying groceries, running errands, part-time employment, or any other need specific to your situation.

When you do your daily planning, check your "Weekly Routines" chart to see whether there's any weekly task you need to account for each day.

Next, make a small chart for the year. Divide it into twelve boxes and label each box with the name of a month. (Refer to Table 7.) Here write down those activities that need to be considered only on a seasonal basis. Go through your notebook looking for these, and enter them appropriately. You may have "Plant the garden" entered in May and June, or "Plan homeschool curriculum" in May and August, or "Wash outside windows and storm windows" in May and October. At the beginning of each month, scan the list of things required to help you remember the types of things you'll need to allot time for in the coming weeks.

Drawing Up Weekly Chore Charts

You may also want to consider using a weekly chore chart, which details the tasks to be performed once a week at those times already assigned in the Weekly Routines charts. I simply wrote out the name of each room at the top of a piece of paper, listed *exactly* the chores that needed to be done in each room every week,

Table 7: Seasonal Activities

January	February	March
Teacher advisory appt.	Household sewing projects	Jessi's birthday
Household sewing projects	Lent	Continue six-week spring cleaning of house
Plan Jan.-May curriculum projects	Begin six-week spring cleaning of house	Income taxes

April	May	June
Anna's birthday	Garden: prune, transplant	Teacher advisory appt.
Mummy's birthday	Wash all bedding, blankets, and curtains	Plant gardens
Plan gardens	Fix screens and clean windows	Buy curriculum
Plan next year's curriculum	Sort summer clothes	Weeding
	Buy curriculum	
	Remove storm windows	

July	August	September
Berries: jams and preserves	Virginia's birthday	Nicki's birthday
Home repair	Plan Sept. – Dec. curriculum	Teacher advisory appt.
Vacation	Prepare house and supplies for new school year	Harvest and freeze food from garden
Begin freezing food from garden		
Weeding		

October	November	December
Yard clean-up	Begin Christmas planning and shopping	Luke's birthday
Sort fall clothes	Begin Christmas baking	Philip's birthday
Prepare winter supplies	Advent preparation	Clean house for Christmas
Install storm windows		

and then assigned a child or my husband or myself to each room. (Refer to Table 8.)

To let the littlest ones help, I circled with a red pen things even a toddler could do, and every cleaning day the children came to me, and I'd read the list and assign them an activity. (They especially love to clean the windows with the spray bottle!) These charts I laminated and posted in the kitchen.

Irregular Concerns

There will be other things that come up, according to the seasons or ages of your children — such as doctor's appointments or seasonal sporting events or even business opportunities — and I suggest that you tackle them as they come. You don't want to account for the sporadic in your Rule. You need to deal only with what's essential, basic, and regular.

Other Important Considerations

On another note, remembering here that we're trying to live a *Rule* and not just a schedule, it's important to try to call to mind at the beginning of each new time frame that you're doing all of this as a response to the call of God. Here, you want to learn to raise your mind and heart to him, offer him all that you do, and ask his blessing on your next scheduled undertaking. You might even want to write out a little prayer and post it above your schedule that you can say when you move into each new activity. Referring to your schedule offers an ideal opportunity to pause for a moment and consecrate this time to him.

Second, but just as important for the success of the Rule, is that it's very difficult to implement a Rule of Life if our home is a mess. The Rule will help *maintain* order, but there has to be at least some level of order established in the first place. Although I suggested

Table 8: Once-a-Week Chores

I list the chores exactly so a child can follow them independently.

Sample: The Living Room

1. Pull out the couch. Pick up any stuff you find there, and put it away *exactly* where it belongs. Vacuum. Push couch back.

2. Do the same for all couches, chairs, and TV stand.

3. Pick up any toys, books, garbage, and anything else from floor, chairs, or tables, and put it away exactly where it belongs.

4. Dust the mantle. Pick up the statues, vases, and candles, and dust under them. Replace them properly.

5. Tidy the bookshelves. Line books up vertically. Dust.

6. Dust TV front and back. Put any videos away properly.

7. Dust the windowsills, and water the plant with 1 cup of water.

8. If needed, wash all windows and TV screen with Windex.

9. Dust my side table, but leave my books (and anything else on it) for me to straighten up.

10. Vacuum room, especially around the edges and behind the door.

11. Mop. Then, with clean, wrung-out mop, rinse the floor.

12. Come ask Mummy what else you need to do, if anything.

you begin your schedule immediately, in whatever capacity possible, it's equally important to set up your home right away by referring to your room analyses. Put everything in the place where you've determined it belongs. Put things you haven't found a place for yet in a temporary holding room, out of the way. Use a basket in the corner to account for something without a special "home." Teach your family where things go, and spend the first week or two supervising this.

If you can't spend three or four days working like a dog to get it all done fast, include in your Rule an initial time when you'll work on home order. This could be Saturdays when you're off work, or you could take advantage of any vacation time, or plan to do it in the afternoons, or you could stop your homeschooling for a week and enlist the aid of your children. You could even hire outside help. The important point is that setting up your home properly is essential to being able to follow your Rule.

Other Uses for Your Notebook

Your notebook can be an ongoing source of organization in your life. You've already recorded any home improvements and repairs that need to be done, so when budgeting and planning your paycheck purchases, you can refer to your notebook to see what can be bought. By having debts listed, you can determine which bill to apply money to.

As you go, you'll find that other areas come up that aren't covered by the previous analysis. Every time a new topic arises — such as Christmas gift lists, vacation ideas, liturgical celebration ideas, personal study topics, or clothing needs — you can set up a new page and keep track of everything you need or want to get down. Write it out, and refer to it when the time comes.

Supernaturalizing Your Rule

From this point forward, then, every time you move into another scheduled event, offer it up to God and ask him for his help and blessing. Place yourself in a spirit of obedience to God's will. Tackle every task as a direct response to God, just as if he were asking you, "Will you go do your laundry now?"

Just say, "Yes, I will." And smile at him. Then you'll be moving ever closer to the heart of your Mother's Rule.

Chapter 9

≈

Getting Determined

I could tell you many more things I've learned about setting up a Mother's Rule of Life. I could tell you to simplify — to get rid of all those extra possessions that are only taking up room in your house and causing you to move stuff around from place to place, day after day.

I could tell you to simplify your activities, too; that being too much "on the go" leaves no room for a peaceful, quiet, and recollected fulfillment of your duties.

I could re-emphasize balance in your daily schedule, encouraging you neither to work too much nor to play too much, but to do all things in moderation and in proper proportion. I could suggest that you work on consistency by beginning with baby steps, taking things slowly, and having patience with your initial meager efforts.

I could also tell you that discouragement, while a very real and seemingly natural possibility, is also a temptation from the very pit of Hell, designed to make you feel bad about yourself and make you afraid to approach God's throne of mercy. I could tell you, when you feel this temptation, to go take a coffee break and to forget about everything for a while until you're ready to try again.

A Mother's Rule of Life

It's Not About Adopting a System

Yes, I could talk to you for six hours, six days, six months; but you still wouldn't be able to go and design, or implement, or maintain your own Mother's Rule. For developing a Rule of Life isn't just about putting together a set of home-management techniques — although these can help. It's not just about being asked just the right questions to answer — although the questions I've already posed for each of the five Ps are good starting points. It's not just about following the right advice.

I can't tell you the number of times I've tried to adopt someone's else's way of organizing and had it fail to work for me; how many times I've been reminded that there's no such thing as an easy fix to bring order into my home and life. That it's not just about choosing a system that I could just implement and then be happy and holy.

Developing my Mother's Rule was dependent on something else, and that something was *me*. Nothing worked for me until the day I got so desperate that I decided to grab my vocation by the horns, tackle it to the ground, and conquer it. I was so frustrated with my life that I had to make a decision. *I had to choose*. As I realized later, it wasn't because my home life was so impossible that I was overwhelmed, even though I felt that way often. It was because I wasn't doing what I *should* have been doing.

There were many reasons, over the course of my marriage. I had personal healing issues that needed to be worked out. I didn't see the importance of child-raising and housework because I was convinced they weren't as important as other things. My head was always in the clouds wishing for something "better." I felt undertrained in the area of home management, despite being well trained in other areas. But primary among the faults that were preventing me from buckling down and living my vocation was *sloth*.

The Insidious Disease of the Will

Even before I began my Rule, I had come upon Fr. John Hardon's striking definition of the deadly sin known as sloth. Sloth is a "sluggishness of soul or boredom of the exertion necessary for the performance of any good work." Yes, I knew what it was like to not want to get up from my chair and bother with my housework. I knew what it meant to be bored with being at home.

"The good work may be a corporal task, such as walking; or a mental task, such as writing; or a spiritual duty, such as prayer." Yes, or cleaning behind the toilet, or balancing my checkbook, or saying the family Rosary!

"Implicit in sloth is the unwillingness to exert oneself in the performance of duty because of the sacrifice and effort required." How many times had I heard myself say, "But I don't *want* to; it will take me forever"?

"As a sin, it is not to be confused with mere sadness over the inconvenience involved in fulfilling one's obligations, nor with the indeliberate feelings of repugnance when faced with unpleasant work. It becomes sinful when the reluctance is allowed to influence the will and, as a result, what should have been done is either left undone or performed less well than a person is responsible for doing."

So if I didn't want to do it, that was one thing, but if I acted upon this feeling, then it became sinful. If I had a habit of not bothering to wash up the dishes after lunch or to make my bed in the morning or to discipline the kids for misbehavior, then when things piled up, I was really seeing only the fruit of my own sloth.

"Sloth can also mean a repugnance to divine inspirations or the friendship of God due to the self-sacrifice and labor needed to cooperate with actual grace or to remain in the state of grace," writes Fr. John Hardon. "This kind of laziness is directly opposed to the love of God and is one of the main reasons why some people, perhaps after years of virtuous living, give up in the pursuit of holiness, or even become estranged from God."

I had to wonder if my inability to find adequate prayer time wasn't more a result of sloth than of being too busy. It seemed I always had enough time to read a book or magazine or watch a show, but prayer was somehow impossible.

I began to realize that sloth is a deadly sin indeed, for it's a disease of the will. It's a spiritual cancer that spreads quietly and unmarked by the patient, all the while eating away at his spiritual vitality. Every time I gave in, even with something as silly as laundry, I was permitting the disease to become more embedded. Sloth could even imperil my eternal salvation. I didn't want to lose my soul over a pile of dirty clothes!

And so I saw a real connection between the state of my soul and the state of my home and family life. Perhaps my vocation wasn't to blame for seeming so impossible; perhaps it was me! I was my own worst enemy.

I later realized that I had come upon all this teaching about sloth throughout that winter of the new millennium, when I thought Jesus wasn't helping me as he'd promised. But he *had* been helping me by revealing to me through my reading a very serious flaw in my soul. I suddenly saw all this as very serious, perhaps for the first time. I was thoroughly convicted — and a bit despairing. How was I to work my way out of this one? I felt too weak.

Remedies for Sloth

I felt weak because I *was* weak. Sloth weakens the will. But there are remedies, things we can do and things God does for us.

First, God wants us to know we're weak. If we don't know this, we'll never realize we need a Savior. The whole world could use a little revelation of this kind. But God doesn't want us to be comfortable with our weakness, nor to use it as an excuse not to try harder. Weakness doesn't lessen or eliminate our calling. What God wants from us is to acknowledge it and turn to him so he can help us. The all-loving, all-knowing, all-present, all-powerful God of the thunderstorm and the volcano and solar flares and supernovas wants to help us in our insignificant little worldly weaknesses! But how?

And as we discussed in the first P, God provides the grace of the sacraments to strengthen our wills. With prayer and frequent reception of the sacraments, especially the Holy Eucharist and Confession, God will begin to give us supernatural strength that will help us rise above the natural limits and weaknesses of our nature.

God helped reveal my slothful tendencies to me through my reading. One of the first things we can do, and one of the primary remedies for sloth, is to strengthen our convictions. We don't bother with things that we don't see as important. But we must realize that work and the responsibilities of the five Ps are very important — so important that our salvation rests on their proper fulfillment. So, a second step involves a vigorous program of study and inquiry to help us value our vocation.

Third, we can train our wills. We discussed this a bit in the "Person" chapter. Our wills, like our muscles, can be exercised and made tougher, more enduring. Every time we consciously choose to follow God's will, to do a good act, we strengthen our own wills and lessen the hold of sloth over our souls. *Every little thing counts every single time.*

And so, instead of looking around the house and saying, "I just can't do *all this,*" I can decide to do something that *is* in my power. I can decide not to have that second piece of cake. I can decide to hug my child. I can decide to give a little more in the Sunday collection. It starts with these little things. Schedule what you can schedule, practice it, do it, and develop a habit. Choose to start that morning prayer time by reading from Scripture. Set your alarm, get up, and grab a cup of coffee. Sit down and read. Just decide to do it. Nothing will change until you do.

Hence, we need to make decisions — to *choose*, consciously and deliberately, to be true to our vocation. This choice alone will enable you to implement a Mother's Rule of Life. I remember my Psychology 101 professor telling us this little story, which I appreciated only later. He told us of a fantastic new Peace Pill that had just been invented. If every leader in the world took the pill, all international disputes would be immediately settled. It seemed like a real answer to the wars and strife in the world, but there was just one little problem: they couldn't figure out how to get the leaders to take the pill.

Likewise, a Mother's Rule of Life will meet many needs and solve many problems in our lives — that is, if we decide to do it and persevere in it. As St. Teresa of Avila once said to her nuns, "What God wants from us is the determination of our wills."

The Problem with Turnips

Turnips aren't supposed to have any worm holes if you want to sell them. This is one of the criteria for having a Canada "Grade A" product. If there's a worm hole, you can trim it with a knife, but not so much that it takes off a big chunk of the skin. If there are big worm holes or if a turnip is over-trimmed, it's considered a cull and is thrown away as unsaleable. But if you have a little tiny worm hole and the rest of the turnip is of good quality, you can still put it in the bag for sale.

Philip grew up on the family farm and often worked with hired crews as they sorted and trimmed the turnips before packaging.

Sometimes he'd see that the cull rate was higher than normal and, upon inspection, would often find perfectly useable turnips in the cull bin. What he eventually realized was that as long as he was totally specific with his instructions, most workers did what they were told, and the cull rate remained normal. But if he forgot to mention something or failed to emphasize a subtle distinction, like the one about the tiny worm holes, many of the crew wouldn't figure it out for themselves, and the job would be done poorly. And as long as they did what they were told, they felt safe from reproach and could rightfully collect their paychecks, despite wasting large amounts of perfectly good turnips.

The problem was that the hired crew hadn't engaged the *meaning* of the process. They were merely walking through the motions, not using their heads. This is a very real possibility when beginning a Mother's Rule as well — to think that once you've made the decision, things will just go smoothly. This calls for a little realism.

In deciding to implement a Rule of Life, we have to engage not only our wills, but also our reason. There are very few problems in our married vocation that prayer and reason cannot eventually master. Immediately after I began my Rule, God stepped in and revealed to me the path he wished me to take, and provided me with grace and understanding to take it. But I also had to *think*, and sometimes think quite hard, so much so that at times I felt as if I had to have a Ph.D. just to be a housewife!

And as with Philip's experience on the farm, this is the difference between being a hired hand and being a son. We mothers aren't hired hands who can simply be told what we must do and blindly follow. No, we're grown women and daughters of the King, and we must act like women and daughters. We must own our responsibilities and take charge of the mission entrusted to us by our Heavenly Father, actively devoting ourselves to fulfilling his will.

This means taking the time to think things through, to fine-tune our Rule, to tinker with schedules and chore charts. Just because things don't pop into place immediately after we decide to do it, doesn't mean there's something wrong. It just means that more thought is required. This is all part of becoming engaged in the process. It could take you years to work out a Rule to your satisfaction, but time is irrelevant. As Mother Teresa once said, "God does not ask us to be successful, only faithful." What counts is that if we fall, we climb back on, use our minds to help us figure out what God is asking, and try again.

Take the Boat Out Again

Peter had been out all night fishing and, having caught nothing, arrived at the dock probably very tired, grumpy, and discouraged. But Jesus told him to take the boat back out and cast out his nets again. Silly. Impossible. Hopeless. Useless. All these words might go through our minds as we try to get our lives in order, perhaps after many failures. But Jesus is asking the same thing of us as he did of Peter: "Put out into deep water, and pay out your nets for a catch."[23] Peter obeyed and caught so many fish that the nets nearly tore.

Taking the step of developing a Mother's Rule of Life can seem like an impossible task if you've been faced with discouragement. Nevertheless, Jesus wants you to fulfill your mission in life, your vocation, and he'll reward your faithful efforts. You'll never catch that boat full of fish if you don't try. So when setbacks come, put your trust in him and say with Peter, "Okay, Lord, I'll try one more time."

[23] Luke 5:4.

Chapter 10

~

The Heart of a Mother's Rule

Now that I look back at it, I was on a pretty rigorous schedule for a beginner. I had divided up my day to cover all the major needs of my vocation. I had regular personal and family prayer scheduled. My meals, housework, and laundry chores were all accounted for. The children's school schedule was briefly worked out. Afternoons were spent on home projects and gardens and so on. I had time set aside just for Philip in the evenings. I had even scheduled in my daily walk, piano playing, and a Sunday manicure!

But there were times in those early weeks and months when I didn't think I was going to make it. In retrospect, I think I started too much too soon, and perhaps should have worked my way into it a bit more gradually. But I was so desperate for change that I just went for it. I felt as if I was working *really* hard.

After my first five days on the Rule, I felt weird — too structured — and looked forward to my Mother's Day Out. But even the day off didn't fully alleviate the pressure, and by the following Monday and Tuesday, I just couldn't follow it anymore. I felt imprisoned — as if I were denying the very person I was by trying to fit myself inside a box. But being off the Rule made me feel even worse! I couldn't bear to go back over the whole "overwhelmed" cycle again.

So by Wednesday, I hopped back into my Rule, and I remember praying at the kitchen counter as I was making lunch: "Dear Jesus, you've got to do something!" Every ounce of my being was fighting just to keep me at the counter instead of sitting down with some coffee and a good book. Every morning I would get up and experience such reluctance and dread in myself that I had to muster up courage with all my might. Yes, all this just to go make my bed when I said I would, and put some breakfast on the table!

And I discovered that I had to accept, again and *again*, that this was what the Lord wanted me to do, just like Jesus in the Garden of Gethsemane. I didn't trust my ability to keep up the fight, because I could feel the tug of sloth and the cringing from effort pull at every part of me. Discouragement would raise its ugly head and threaten to engulf me. I realized I needed more grace.

I found a little quote in Adolphe Tanquerey's *The Spiritual Life* that I wrote out and posted above the sink:

> As to the virtues, it's evident that they must continue to cultivate them, particularly those that are proper to their state in life . . . in a state of holy abandonment into the hands of God; and if they go about this courageously, this state of soul will prove a goldmine which will yield great profits.

Whenever I got discouraged, aside from storming Heaven with my pleas for help, I'd go and read this little quote to help me to persevere.

I eventually went to my spiritual director as well and asked him to place me under obedience. I showed him a copy of my Rule; he examined it and said he thought it was reasonable. That was important to me, because I didn't want my resolve weakened by vague temptations to think that I was overdoing it. So he told me that if I wanted, I could follow my Rule under obedience to him as my director, as well as under obedience to the demands of my calling.

Well, what a change that made! St. Teresa of Avila was right: obedience brings strength. I felt filled with strength. Suddenly my life was full of details and full of meaning, and it all became exciting and challenging. I went day by day, figuring out what had to be done with all the little details I hadn't accounted for yet, and how and when I could do them. Everything was in order. My stress level dropped considerably. The kids were all busy and active. My work was getting done. I had a real and regular prayer life. The benefits were all exhilarating, at least for a while, for as is customary with God, he was calling me to an even deeper level.

Getting to the Heart of the Mother's Rule

When I first began working on my Rule, I think in my heart I was mostly interested in doing it for my benefit — to bring order to my life and reduce the frustration. But one day, a few months after I had begun, I woke up and I was *bored*. Day after day, the boredom didn't go away. You see, I had solved the problem; I had conquered the challenge; I had overcome the obstacles. By gosh, I was practically perfect! But now, there was nothing left to think about.

"Humph," I thought. "Is this all there is to life? Am I going to live out the rest of my days in boredom?" I knew I couldn't stop this and move on to something else because I still had a vocation to live, and my family and home weren't going to go away.

And so, quite uneventfully, one day while I was standing at the kitchen counter, I thought, "Maybe I could start doing every little thing for the love of God. Maybe I could just start offering everything up to him. This would surely help my soul, wouldn't it?"

And so I began.

The first day I tried this, I was blown away by how regularly I *didn't* do things for God. Every time I said, "Jesus, I do this for love of you," it felt strange and foreign to me. I realized that I needed to work on this, and the best way was just to practice it. So I began to fold that baby sleeper "just so" for love of Jesus. I washed the table as if Jesus were coming to supper. I hugged my children as if they were Jesus himself. And I began to accept all that happened to me as coming from the hands of my loving, all-good God. I began to submit myself to him and his will in my life.

And the most amazing, most wonderful thing happened: God came! God *really* came! And he popped in at the most extraordinary moments. I'd be folding laundry and be overwhelmed by his presence. I'd be weeding the garden, and my soul would be filled with a profound peace and stillness. I'd be scrubbing dishes and experience a closer union with God than I'd ever experienced in my formal prayer time. I'd be in front of the Blessed Sacrament and feel what I called a "tractor beam" pulling my heart in the middle of my chest toward Jesus! It was all the strangest thing.

I ran back to my Tanquerey book and found something that made my heart rise in gratitude to God. I was experiencing a form of contemplation. Oh, not the silent contemplation that a religious in a quiet convent might experience, but a contemplation tailor-made to mothers:

> [S]ince the will alone is held captive [by God], the other faculties are free to attend to things relating to God's service; and this they do with far greater energy. Then, when the soul is engaged in exterior works, it continues to love God ardently; this is the union of action and contemplation, of the service of Martha and the love of Mary.

So I learned that contemplation is a form of prayer where God seizes hold of the will and fills it with peace and quietude and strength. God had given me the strength I had so desperately needed and asked for.

This is called *active contemplation*, and I figure it was designed especially by God so that busy moms could experience it, too! My earlier doubts about whether one could become truly holy or really reach God as a married person were erased, as I saw opening before me the hope that, hey, I might just get closer to God through this marriage thing after all.

Disposing Ourselves to Contemplation

God calls all souls to contemplation because he *wants* to give himself to us, to unite himself with us intimately. But this form of prayer is a free gift of God and isn't something acquired by our own efforts. We can't control God and "make" him give us extraordinary graces even if we've been "very good"; he'd be no more than a glorified Santa Claus. We can't command his mystical presence, nor can we produce such contemplation on demand. It's instead a presence and action of God himself, something "infused" into us, given or not given at a time of his choosing, not ours.

To illustrate, picture yourself standing at the edge of a cliff after a long, rigorous journey, having done all in your power to get to where you were going. But now there's no more road; only a vast ocean spreads out before you. You're perplexed; you worked so hard climbing that mountain to get to God, but you've found only what seems like a dead end. Then you look up, and you realize that your goal is not of this world, but somewhere else: the moon! You see the futility of all your efforts; you feel brought to a standstill; there's no way you can get to the moon on your own steam. Only if a rocket ship comes down and picks you up will you ever get there.

Infused prayer is just like this. Despite all our efforts, there's nothing we can do to bring about any sublime, mystical union with God on our own steam or by our own virtue. No, God himself must intervene and lift us up to him with *his* power, not ours.

And for this reason St. Teresa of Avila considered it a *supernatural* prayer, explaining, "I call supernatural that which cannot be acquired either by industry or by effort, no matter what pains we take for the purpose. As to disposing oneself thereto, this indeed one can do, and this is no doubt a great thing."[24] So although we can't earn contemplation, we can *dispose* ourselves to it.

How? Since contemplation is a prayer within the heart, our response to God must be from the heart: *by surrendering ourselves to him and by accepting wholeheartedly his will for us;* by repeating with the Blessed Mother, "Behold, the handmaid of the Lord. Be it done unto me according to thy word"; by seeking to love and please God; by living out our Mother's Rule: accepting our vocation as God's will, and seeking to dedicate ourselves completely to its fulfillment, simply because he wants us to, because we love him. This is how we dispose ourselves.

St. Faustina said, "On one occasion, Jesus gave me to know how pleasing to him is the soul that faithfully keeps the Rule. A soul will receive a greater reward for observing the Rule than for penances and great mortifications. The latter will be rewarded also if they are undertaken over and above the Rule, but they will not surpass the Rule."

St. Teresa of Avila said, "Let us understand, my daughters, that true perfection consists in love of God and neighbor. . . . All that is in our Rule . . . serves for nothing else than to be a means toward keeping these commandments with greater perfection."

[24] Quoted in Tanquerey, *The Spiritual Life,* 650.

To Love God

The fulfillment of our Mother's Rule in fidelity to God's designs for us as women, wives, and mothers is an act of love for God. But it must become more than an act of the will; it must develop into a movement of the heart. God is not satisfied with a mere external observance. He wants our hearts as well, and over time, we need to see the obedience of our relationship with God transform into the love necessary for intimacy with him. I once heard that St. Thérèse of Lisieux's "little way" was based on a very simple premise: *just fall in love with Jesus and seek to please him.*

How, as busy moms, can we practically initiate this? We can begin, more and more, to offer up to God every little thing we do as an act of love for him: "Jesus, I do this because I love you." We can perform each task, as it presents itself to us at any given moment, with the greatest care and solicitude.

We can slowly learn to focus on each moment with our full attention — applying body, soul, and mind — and recall that everything, no matter how small or routine is permitted by God to bring us closer to him. Realizing that God acts in the present moment, not in the future nor the past, but only *now*, we can be open and attentive to his whisperings, and accept all that happens to us as coming from the loving hands of our heavenly Father for our own *good*. These are the attitudes of the heart necessary to love God within our Rule.

And so although contemplation is a free gift, nevertheless (as St. Teresa of Avila said), "Love attracts Love." Our generosity toward God attracts his generosity toward us, and God will not be outdone in generosity. This singleness of purpose — *consciously doing God's will because it is his will, and out of love for him* — is also known as purity of heart, and it paves the way for contemplation. It's the Sixth Beatitude: "Blessed are the pure in heart, for they shall see God."[25] It is, in fact, our own imitation of Christ, who was obedient to the Father's will, out of love, even to his own death on the Cross.

As St. Faustina said, "Only one thing is needed to please God: to do even the smallest things out of great love — love and always love."

The Heart of the Rule Is Contemplation

Before my Rule, when all I could think about was how in the world I was ever going to get the house clean, I had no mental space for thinking of anything else. When I was constantly living my life based on my desires and whims of the moment, I had no room in my heart for God. There were always more than enough things to fill my affections and my attention. A home and a life in disorder lead to "dissipation" — a scattering of our interior faculties — and prevent us from becoming still enough to listen to God speaking inside us.

But it was only when I reached the point of getting bored, after my Rule was established, that I was free enough to open my mind and heart to God; to be internally attentive to him and to be conscious of doing all for the love of him. It was *then* that I experienced his profound presence, which, in turn, inspired a new love for my family. So a Mother's Rule leads to recollection: that deep calm and quiet of the interior life of our souls. Freed from outside concerns, we become more peaceful, more in touch with our inner nature, and we discover our hearts. There we encounter an entirely new possibility of frequent conversation with God and a deeper communion with him. I think this is part of John the Baptist's call to us to level the mountains of cares and anxieties, to fill

[25] Matt. 5:8.

in the valleys of busyness and details, and to make a straight path for the Lord.[26]

I've often heard it said that everything we do is prayer; that simply to live is prayer; and this is true — but only when we're conscious of it; and we're conscious of it when our lives are in order and free from unnecessary concerns. As Dom Chautard says in *The Soul of the Apostolate:* "Let the following conviction become deeply impressed upon your mind: namely, that a soul cannot lead an interior life without a *schedule . . .* and without a *firm resolution* to keep it all the time." For this reason, a Mother's Rule seems to be very much a necessary prerequisite to contemplation in our daily lives. And contemplation, remember, is the experience of God himself.

The Blessed Benefit of Our Purification

When I was a little girl, I was in the hospital for an extended period. One day my mother brought me a little poster for my hospital room that said, "Have patience with me; God isn't finished with me yet."

This poster was prophetic for me, as I think it is for all of us. God is never finished with us. Yes, I thought I was practically perfect, but God didn't leave me there. After he led me to the challenge of struggling to conform my will to his will, to turn my heart to his heart, then *he* began the challenge of purifying me from the inside out.

When we try to love God, God himself comes to visit us. He comes with gifts of joy and peace and consolation, to show us he's pleased and to enable us to set out on this path. But He also sends us these enabling graces in their arid forms, because when we

[26] Cf. Matt. 3:3.

reach this level of the *heart,* we begin clearly to realize that God still has more work to do. He wants to purge the roots of sin and vice so that he alone may occupy our hearts.

And, in fact, the purgative action of grace in our hearts is the very same presence of God that we experience in consoling and sweet contemplation. It's just that we subjectively perceive the action of God differently at different times. For God comes to *enkindle us with fire* — the fire of love and the fire of purification, and both are the same *fire of God.*

With the arid form, one can undergo a spiritual pain incomparable in intensity, but so infused with love as to enable us even to embrace the pain. St. Teresa of Avila often talked about the "wound of love" that she considered a delectable pain, something so precious that she didn't want it to end.

This is what St. John of the Cross calls the Dark Night of the Spirit, when God goes to our deepest core and readies our hearts for union. It's very important for us to remember that with every presence of God in our hearts that purifies, there's a corresponding inpouring of love to enable us to bear it. God stretches and pulls our hearts of stone to make them flesh, and it *hurts!* But, at this point, pain becomes enwrapped, permeated, and infused with a love that burns like fire, fueling a deep and living intimacy with God.

So, when we experience pain and a little voice tempts us to turn back, let us say with St. Peter, "Lord, to whom shall we go?"[27] Let us say with Mary, "Behold the handmaid of the Lord. Be it done unto me according to thy word."[28] Let us say, "Lord give me a willing heart and a docile spirit."

[27] John 6:68.
[28] Luke 1:38.

Sharing Christ's Burden

There's something else we can do with the suffering we experience. We can join our sufferings to Christ's, to "make up in our own bodies what is still lacking in the sufferings of Jesus," as St. Paul says.[29]

Part of our Christian mission, part of our very imitation of Christ, is to accept all that comes to us from the hands of a loving God, and to offer it up to the Father, in union with the sufferings of Jesus. We who make up the Mystical Body of Christ can participate in the redemptive Passion for the conversion and salvation of the world. We can take all the little or great struggles in trying to live our vocation, all the trials and tribulations of our purification, and offer these back to the Father with Jesus in order to help those who may not be free enough to help themselves.

The Choice Is Yours

The Christian life is never easy. I know at some points in my life I've seen it as totally repulsive. What could we expect from a Savior who says, "Take up your cross, deny yourself, and follow me"?[30] It's never pleasant to ponder the possibility of suffering either. But I've discovered in my life that suffering is bound to come one way or another, so I might as well make it count for something now, shouldn't I?

And, of course, a Rule of Life is certainly not just about suffering. It's about personal balance and loving relationships and intimacy with God. After a very intense first year or so, I began to notice a real improvement in my ability to meet the demands of my vocation. Things weren't so hard anymore. After two years, I

[29] Cf. Col. 1:24.
[30] Cf. Matt. 16:24.

realized that somewhere along the line, without my noticing it, I'd experienced a real calming of my person; I no longer had big ups or downs. I'd get up in the morning, and I'd be ready to start my day without any of the earlier reluctance or difficulty. My home was usually in satisfactory order, and the kids' schooling was coming along very well. That has continued until the present time, and it's coming on four years. I've even had time to write this book without its normally cutting in on any other responsibilities (although I feel busier than usual!).

But most important, I've time for God and for my family. I can truly love them and attend to them. I know now that the most important things are the relationships God has placed in my life. I could say a whole new world has opened up for me, one that I had never discovered before, and I like it. Not that everything's perfect, but it's better. It's good.

Despite all the struggles, I feel as if God has done me a tremendous service. All those times he came to visit me, I was strengthened. All those times he purified me, well, he got rid of a lot of garbage in my soul. But now I feel free — free to love my God, my husband, and my kids, and free to do what I need to do without being burdened by it.

I wish for you the same freedom. So consider whether you, too, are called to live your own Mother's Rule of Life. Think and pray hard about it. Don't limit your discernment to whether you want a clean house. This won't motivate anyone for very long. And don't bring up all your faults and weaknesses at once, or you'll never think clearly enough to even begin. And believe that if God wants you to do it, he'll empower you.

Do you desire more order in your life? Do you want to be a better wife and mother? Are you looking for a deeper relationship with God? Are you desperate yet?

God may well be asking you, in this era of marital and family decline, to make this conscious, wholehearted commitment to him and to your family as part of a renewal of the world. May God be with you.

Appendix

⁀⁀

The Spirit of the Mother's Rule

As we discussed in chapter 2, the spirit of your Rule of Life — its underlying philosophy and goals — is even more important than the practical schedules. In fact, without a spiritual guide, your practical Rule will tend to be more confusing and more difficult to follow.

Over time, I've worked out the spirit of my Rule and put it down on paper. I recommend you do the same. The spirit of your Rule will summarize the main points of how you want to live out your vocation, based on the five Ps, the specific virtues you believe most important to your vocation and unique circumstances, and the particular goals, attitudes, and frames of mind and heart you believe God is calling you to.

The spirit of your Rule is meant to be a goal and guide, an objective, something that you work toward — *not* something you'll accomplish perfectly right off the bat. In her diary, St. Faustina used to keep track of how many times she failed in her Rule! So if a saint has to try, we shouldn't expect perfection either. The spirit of the Rule is meant not for discouragement, but for encouragement.

Writing out the spirit of your Rule will help you regularly re-examine how well you're adhering to your Rule overall. It's normal for some religious to do an examination of their fidelity to the

A Mother's Rule of Life

Rule every month, as part of an overall "spiritual health" program. I do something like that fairly regularly, and most thoroughly every autumn when I go to reassess the schedule. And when I find things confusing, or I find I have no vigor, I go and reread the spirit of my Rule. I find it helps to pull my often wayward heart back on track, and calls to mind just what I'm supposed to be doing on this earth anyway!

So, over the course of the next few months, start jotting down what you consider the essential points of what God is calling you to as a Christian, woman, wife, and mother. This will be the spirit of your Rule.

Below I've included the spirit of my Mother's Rule of Life for you to use as a helpful model.

The Spirit of My Mother's Rule of Life

In seeking Christian perfection
within the married vocation, as I
repeat with the Blessed Mother:

"Behold the handmaid of the Lord.
Be it done unto me according to thy word."

Underlying all that I do, I will aim to focus on the purpose of my vocation, and live the *heart* of the Mother's Rule:

The Will of God

I will faithfully fulfill the will of God in my life by the living out of the duties and responsibilities of my vocation. This necessitates:

• An ongoing study of the duties of my state in life as reflected in the five Ps, with the intent to implement discoveries in my daily life.

• The development and practice of a basic, general schedule to ensure the accomplishment of all essential duties, and the proper and efficient use of my time.

• The reduction or removal of excessive outside involvements or ministries or companions if they interfere in any ongoing way with my ability to fulfill my duties in recollection and serenity.

The Love of God

I will attempt to do *all* for the love of God, as opposed to following my own inclinations and motives. To this end:

• I call to mind the reasonableness of my rule as it fulfills God's will for me, and so I accept *wholeheartedly* my scheduled tasks.

• I begin, more and more, to offer up each task to God for the love of God alone, as my *sole motivation*.

• I perform *each* task, no matter what, with the *greatest care and solicitude* and tenderness, *as it presents itself to me at that moment*, for I am performing it as an act of love for God, who is with me.

• I am fully focused on *the present moment*, and the task at hand — applying body, soul, and mind — as I recall that *all* that happens to me is permitted by God in order to bring me closer to him.

• I am open and *receptive to the promptings of the Holy Spirit*, awaiting his whisper at each moment, and I practice acceptance, patience, and thanksgiving both in joys and in trials.

A Mother's Rule of Life

The Love of Neighbor

I will attempt actively to love my neighbor, especially my husband and my children, looking within each person for Christ himself, who dwells there, and all of my actions, words, and thoughts will be done "with Christ, for Christ, and to Christ." To this end:

- I will be *externally and internally available* to my family and all in genuine need, by ceasing unnecessary tasks to respond to them, and by controlling the busyness of my heart and head to listen carefully.

- I will be *attentive* to the person I am presently with, leaving them with the impression that they are the only person in the world who matters at any given moment.

- I will be *accepting and encouraging* of each person's self and concerns, and I will look for the good within each person.

- I will be *helpful* in any appropriate capacity to all, according to the set priorities of my state in life.

- I will seek to *do what is best* for others and to bring out the best in others.

- I will seek to be firm yet gentle, cheerful, kind, and just, all with tenderness and mercy.

Key Aspects of My Mother's Rule

- I will bring about and maintain *order* with time, possessions, and desires, for only orderliness will enable my heart to be recollected and leave room in my heart for the contemplation of God.

• I will focus on *simplicity* — filling my life, my heart, my head, and my home with nothing that will distract me from the pursuit of God's will in my life. This includes:

> • *Simplicity of possessions:* regularly rethinking and reducing excessive or unnecessary goods that I own in a spirit of detachment as suits family life.

> • *Simplicity of activities:* reducing and refusing superfluous activity that only stresses and crowds daily life; I will focus on a simple list of essentials and on their serene fulfillment.

> • *Simplicity in virtue:* not concerning myself with attaining this or that specific virtue, I will aim solely at finding out what God wants and fulfilling this out of love for him.

• I will practice *moderation* in all things, so that all that I do is balanced and never excessive, reflected in all areas of life — food and recipes, clothing, prayer, work, recreation, exercise, and appearance.

• I will pay careful *attention to detail* in all that I do, so that all things will be well done and with care, but avoiding at the same time a perfectionism that strives to please my whims and not God's design.

• I will be *flexible* with the schedule itself; the times given being general and approximate guides for what is to happen next. Although my adherence to these norms must be firm, I must permit the appropriate flexibility necessitated by the needs of my family. Flexibility is determined by *real* needs, not mere convenience or "not feeling like it" today.

• I will reflect upon the spirit of my Mother's Rule regularly in order to examine my fidelity to it.

The Five Ps

I will be faithful to the fulfillment of the five Ps in my life and seek to practice the spirit of each P fully. To this end:

• I will spend time with God every day, throughout my day, both in formal prayer times and in seeking his presence in each moment as I become able to foster recollection in my heart. I will make use of the standard practices of the Church on a regular basis to maintain my spiritual vigor and purity, including the sacraments, Adoration, spiritual counsel, regular retreat and reflection days, as well as study and prayer groups if these are available. I will offer myself and my joys and sufferings with any merits to the Lord and the Blessed Mother for them to apply them as they see fit.

• I will spend time examining my life and my person and seek the necessary means to bring about my own personal health, both in body and in mind, and commit to a regular examination of my motives and reasons for why I am as I am, with a determination to overcome my most obvious fault or weakness. I will seek to bring about personal internal order by using my reason and guard against random erroneous thoughts, and by choosing always to do the good in any given situation. I will pray for God's grace to heal and convert my heart, and to fill it with his love.

• I will actively love my husband, and according to the special consecration inherent in the sacrament of Marriage, I accept as my mission the encouragement, support, and love of his person over my own selfish desires or whims. I will help him in any way I can.

• I will actively love my children according to the mission entrusted me by God himself. I will do this by:

> • A kind and generous demeanor, encouraging words and loving tone, and in all that I say or reveal by my actions, a pride in their persons, their goodness, and their dignity.

> • Careful attendance to their physical needs, by ensuring a functional and orderly home, good nutrition, and proper physical hygiene and fitness.

> • Careful attendance to their religious and moral formation, assuming the responsibility of teaching and training them, providing regular access to prayer and the sacraments, and witnessing a Christian worldview by both example and words.

> • Careful attendance to the formation of their persons, by ensuring proper academic formation, the development of their particular gifts and talents, and attentive supervision in all areas of life, especially media use and appropriate companions.

• I will be a steward of the possessions and resources God has given me, and use them to fulfill the mission of meeting the spiritual and human needs of my family first, and then, if applicable, by attending to the needs of those less fortunate than I, placing all at the service of God and people, and not claiming as my own any excessive use of goods for my own pleasure, luxury, or personal satisfaction. I will strive for Christian detachment in this area.

Dedication to the Rule

• To ensure a proper fulfillment of my vocational responsibilities, I will review my Rule at a set point each year, adapting it to the needs of my growing or diminishing family.

• I will fulfill my Rule out of a spirit of obedience to the will of God, to the demands of my vocation, or if I wish, I can present it to my spiritual director, to have the added benefit and blessing of obedience to him.

Bibliography

Attwater, Donald, ed. *A Catholic Dictionary*. New York: The Macmillan Company, 1943.

Catechism of the Catholic Church, Libreria Editrice Vaticana. St. Paul, Minnesota: The Wanderer Press, 1994.

Chautard, Dom Jean-Baptiste, O.C.S.O. *The Soul of the Apostolate*. Trappist, Kentucky: Abbey of Gethsemani, Inc., 1946.

Chrysostom, St. John. *On Living Simply: The Golden Voice of John Chrysostom*. Compiled by Robert Van de Weyer. Liguori, Missouri: Liguori / Triumph Publications, 1996.

Cullinane, Eugene. *Don Stefano Comes to Combermere: The Marian Movements Meet*. Combermere, Ontario: Madonna House, c. 1984.

De Hovre, Rev. Franz, Ph.D. *Catholicism in Education*. Translated by Rev. Edward B. Jordan, MA, St.D. New York: Benzinger Brothers, 1934.

Dunney, Joseph A. *The Parish School*. New York: Macmillan Co., 1921.

Gjergji, Lush. *Mother Teresa: Her Life, Her Works*. Hyde Park, New York: New City Press, 1991.

Hardon, John A., S.J. *Pocket Catholic Dictionary*. New York: Doubleday Image Books, 1985.

Hardon, John A., S.J. *The Catholic Catechism*. Garden City, New York: Doubleday and Company, Inc., 1975.

John of the Cross. *Dark Night of the Soul* in *The Collected Works of St. John of the Cross*. Translated by Kieran Kavanaugh, OCD and Otilio Rodriguez, OCD. Washington, D.C.: ICS Publications (Institute of Carmelite Studies), 1979.

John Paul II. *Salvifici Doloris (On the Christian Meaning of Human Suffering)*. 11 February 1984. Vatican translation. Boston: Daughters of St. Paul.

John Paul II. 2002 World Youth Day. Television broadcast, Toronto, Canada: CBC Television, 2002.

Kowalska, St. Faustina. *Divine Mercy in My Soul*. Stockbridge, Massachusetts: Marian Press, 1987, 1990.

Landon, Joseph FGS. *The Principles and Practice of Teaching and Classroom Management*. London: Edinburgh University Press, 1902.

Maxwell, Steve and Teri. *Managers of Their Homes: A Practical Guide to Daily Scheduling for Christian Home-School Families*. Leavenworth, Kansas: Communication Concepts, Inc., 1998, 1999.

Paul VI. *Evangelii Nuntiandi (Evangelization in the Modern World)*. 8 December 1975. In Austin Flannery OP, ed., *Vatican Council II: More Post Conciliar Documents*. Northport, New York: Costello Publishing Co., 1982.

Pius XI. *Christian Education of Youth*. Washington, D.C.: National Catholic Welfare Conference, 1930.

Sheen, Msgr. Rev. Fulton. *Love, Marriage and Children* from the *Life Is Worth Living* series. New York: Dell Publishing Co., Inc., 1957.

Tanquerey, Rev. Adolphe, SS, DD. *The Spiritual Life: A Treatise on Ascetical and Mystical Theology*. Translated by Rev. Herman Branderis, SS, DD. Tournai, Belgium: Society of St. John the Evangelist, Desclée and Co. Publishers, c. 1930.

Teresa of Avila. *Autobiography* in *The Life of Teresa of Jesus: The Autobiography of Teresa of Avila*. Translated and edited by E. Allison Peers. New York: Doubleday Image Books, 1991.

Teresa of Avila, *The Interior Castle* in *The Collected Works of St. Teresa of Avila*, Volume 2. Translated by Kieran Kavanaugh, OCD and Otilio Rodriguez, OCD. Washington, D.C.: ICS Publications (Institute of Carmelite Studies), 1980.

Holly Pierlot

Holly Pierlot was born in 1961 and grew up in Fredericton, New Brunswick, Canada. In her late teens, after dropping out of university, she entered the music business as a vocalist and keyboardist. After a powerful reconversion to Catholicism, she left the road and returned to school. There she met Philip, her husband, and they both became teachers. Eventually circumstances and providence led to a move to Prince Edward Island, where Holly now lives with her husband and her five children, whom she homeschools.

Over the years, in addition to serving as catechetics director of a large Catholic parish, Holly has been actively involved in the homeschooling movement on Prince Edward Island. Today she is a popular speaker at homeschooling conferences and parish marriage and catechetics programs.